CRUEL FATE

CRUEL FATE

One Man's Triumph Over Injustice

HUGH CALLAGHAN

and Sally Mulready

POOLBEG

First published 1993
This edition January 1994
by Poolbeg
A division of Poolbeg Enterprises Ltd
Knocksedan House
123 Baldoyle Industrial Estate
Dublin 13

© Hugh Callaghan and Sally Mulready 1993

The moral rights of the authors have been asserted.

A catalogue record for this book is available from the British Library.

ISBN 1 85371 323 6

Cover photograph John Potter, Newsteam International
Cover design by Poolbeg Group Services Ltd
Set by Mac Book Ltd
Printed by The Guernsey Press Company Ltd,
Vale, Guernsey, Channel Islands.

To our entire legal team, who rescued us from hell

ACKNOWLEDGEMENTS

To my wife, Eileen, for her unstinting loyalty and her heroic work on behalf of us all. To Geraldine and Arthur for their love and affection. To my sister Patsy, who kept faith with me and wrote so many encouraging letters. To my brothers Noel, Charlie and Dan and my late brother Tom.

To the incomparable Gareth Peirce I pay my warmest tribute. Without her we might never have known freedom. To Mike Mansfield QC, Tony Gifford QC and Richard Ferguson QC for their personal commitment to our cause. To Ivan Geffen, solicitor, for his invaluable assistance to all of us.

To Father Denis Faul, Father Brady and Father Raymond Murray for their courageous pamphlet: *The Birmingham Framework*, written shortly after our convictions. It was the first public document to declare our innocence! I was profoundly moved by their work.

To Chris Mullin MP for his book *Error of Judgement*, which positively influenced successive Home Secretaries, judges, lawyers, cardinals, bishops, police officers, and many of his sceptical colleagues in Parliament.

To Charles Tremyne, Ian McBride and Ray Fitzwalter of the *World in Action* Granada television programmes, which broke the story to millions of viewers.

To ex-PCs Tom Clarke and Joyce Lynas and PC Fred Willoughby for coming forward at a crucial time in our struggle and for their tremendous courage. I deeply appreciate what they and several other police officers did to assist us.

To Sir John Farr for his integrity and commitment to establishing the truth, I will remain immensely grateful.

To Jean and Denis Murphy from Belfast, true friends who from 1975 to my release stood by me and in a very special way helped me to "do my bird."

To Séamus Kelters and the Belfast *Irish News* for their generous encouragement over several years.

To the *Irish Post*, the now retired editor, Breandán Mac Lua, Paul Gribben, Terry Smith and Mel and Malcolm McNally for their years of excellent coverage of our fight.

To Michael Farrell, who wrote and campaigned endlessly for us and other victims of miscarriages of justice.

To Dr McKeith and Dr Gudjonsson for their help, encouragement and kindness to me.

To all the people who joined the campaign groups all over the world I say a special thank you. Without your help and the massive campaign conducted on our behalf, the legal establishment and the police would have continued to deny our innocence.

Especially to Paul May for the outstanding leadership he gave to the campaigns in Britain. To Anita Richards and Sue Milner, who worked in the hostile atmosphere of Birmingham for several years. I acknowledge their great work and courage. To Breda Power, Maggie McIlkenny and Paddy McIlkenny for their terrific spirit and fight on behalf of our families and the six of us. To Toni Price and Annie Blindell for their superb newsletter.

To David Andrews TD, Niall Andrews MEP, Peter Barry TD, Dick Roche TD, Senator Paschal Mooney, Séamus Mallon MP, John Hume MP, Jo Richardson MP, Jeremy Corbyn MP, Harry Cohen MP, Tony Benn MP, Alex Carlisle MP, Christine Crawley MEP, Gerald Kaufman MP, Chris Smith MP, Clive Soley MP, Claire Short MP, and all the MPs who supported the early day's motions in the House of Commons arranged by Chris Mullin and Jeremy Corbyn.

To Senators Edward and Joe Kennedy, Courtney Kennedy, Sandy Boyer (New York), Kathy Lisowski (Brooklyn, Massachusetts), and Roger Poirier (San Francisco). To the several US and state congressmen and senators who made representations on our behalf. Their taking up our fight throughout America was enormously significant and embarrassed the British legal establishment in the eyes of the whole world. I deeply appreciate their help. I wish to mention in particular Frank Doris, state senator from Massachusetts, US Congressman Ben Gillman, Congressman Hamilton Fish, and Ray Flynn, former mayor of Boston. To Seán and Frank McManus, who used their considerable influence in the Irish-American community to broadcast our plight.

To Sister Sarah Clarke, a good friend and a comfort to many Irish prisoners in English prisons. She has my deepest respect and admiration.

To Mike Walsh, who gave help and advice to Eileen and the other wives at the very start of our struggle.

To Nuala Kelly of the Irish Commission for Prisoners Overseas for years of good work on our behalf and on behalf of all Irish prisoners abroad. To the Relatives' Action Group in Belfast, who assisted our relatives in a very special way, especially to Sister Caitríona and Joan Knowles. I also say thank you to my friends in Belfast, especially Paddy Cassidy,

Mary Mallon, and Mrs and Mr Kelters.

To Father Joe Taaffe, Father Bobby Gilmore, Father Paddy Smith, Father Jim Kiely and Carmel Murphy of the Irish Chaplaincy for their help and encouragement. To the Columban Fathers, who welcomed us into their house immediately after our release.

To the people of Dublin who came out onto the streets in support of us. Special thanks to the Dublin campaign committee and to those good people who held a weekly vigil outside the British embassy since 1978. My sincere thanks to Jim Hackett and Mrs Medhbh O'Colman who despite their seniority in years never missed a week at the embassy. To Cardinal Hume and his staff, who continued to work behind the scenes on behalf of us and other innocent Irish people, I thank them sincerely.

To Bishop Edward Daly for his compassion and his concern.

To Bishop Victor Guazzelli of east London and Bishop John Crowley I say a special thanks for all their efforts. To Father Hugh Sinclair and Sister Agnes Hunt for their kindness to me during my stay in Wormwood Scrubs.

I would like especially to thank the following people, many of whom suffered with us: Sandra Hunter, Patsy Power, Nora Power, Betsy Power, Mrs Eileen Hoctor, Bernadette Walker, Kate McIlkenny, Pat Hill, Brian and Lilly Kelly, and Teresa McIlkenny.

To Heather Mills of the *Independent* for her friendship and support. To Nuala Ó Faoláin, Carol Coulter and the journalists of the *Irish Times* who kept the judges on their toes with their superb coverage of the '87 and '91 appeals.

To Paul Foot of the *Daily Mirror* and Richard Ingrams of the *Observer*, who harped continuously on the theme of our innocence. To the Birmingham journalist Gerry Hunt for his courage and persistence. To Oscar Gilligan, Jürgen Schneider and Ralf Sotscheck for their brilliant book, *An Appalling Vista*.

To Bob Dawson, treasurer of the London campaign, who arranged financial assistance for our families during the long appeal hearings in London in '87 and '91.

To Jeremy Hardy, Christy Moore, Brush Shields, Cyril Maguire, Mary Black, Billy Steven, Kit Hollerbach and the many performers and artists who gave their services so freely on our behalf in venues all over Britain and Ireland.

To Gloria and Éamonn Kiernan of the GAA in London, who raised thousands of pounds for our campaign. To Michael Clifford, who walked from Birmingham to Downing Street as his special gesture of support. To my good friend Keith Twitchell, who was a great person to talk to in the bad times in prison.

There were many good people who wrote, joined campaigns and did an enormous amount of work to assist us in our struggle. To Eileen's good friends who stood by her and gave her great support in her troubled times, May Beck, Mary Pearson, and Angela Roach, who put Eileen up on her many visits to the Scrubs in London. To Margaret Duffy and John McCabe and to all their families, who were a tremendous help to Eileen. Kathleen Doody, Margaret Szabo, Joanna Roache, Father Denis Cormican, Father Bedlow, Paddy Bond, John Woodhurst, Deirdre Collins, Eithne Grant, Maureen Ó Muimhneacháin, Eithne Doyle from Dublin, and Paul Murray (Irish Embassy). To Seán Healy, Felix Maguire, Sister Joan Kane, Tommy Walsh, Steve McCabe, Jack Kennedy, Andy Higgins, Annie O'Halloran, Phil and Michael Brosnan (Tralee), Val Vaness, Conor Ryan, Seán Brady, Billy Steven, Frank Foley, Paudie Lynch, Seán Furlong, Jane Doolan, Bruce Kent, Brian Deasy, and JM O'Neill. To the Sisters of St Gilda, Crouch End, London, who accommodated many of the families during the

'91 appeal. To Bactia and Angela Harmoz and Chris Berry, who drove our families to and from the Court of Appeal in '87 and '91. To those whose names I do not know, who helped in any small way, I also say a very sincere thank you.

With sincere gratitude to the trade unions whose substantial financial donations greatly assisted the campaigns in their work. The most generous of these were NALGO, UCATT, HUM, and the NUT. A special thanks to Terry Luke and Caroline Hall of NALGO.

To John Wain, my probation officer at Long Lartin—a good man.

To Father Colm Ó Gallchóir, Fr Jimmy Walsh, Fr Bernie Costello, Fr Dermot Dunne, Mrs Babs Kelly and Janet Rowland for their kindness and assistance to Eileen and me after my release.

To Séamus and Sally Mulready I express my enormous gratitude for all their generous support to my family before and since my release. I say thanks also to them and their children Molly, Nora, Ned and Séamie for making Eileen and me so welcome into their home during the writing of this book.

I pay a special tribute to Sally, who helped me to complete this work. She encouraged and inspired me especially through difficult times. Her friendship and support were invaluable to me.

I would like to especially honour and acknowledge the support and companionship of my five co-defendants, Billy, Paddy, Dick, Gerry, and John.

Finally to all innocent prisoners still struggling for justice and freedom: may they never be forgotten.

CONTENTS

FOREWORD

Hugh Callaghan was the unluckiest of the six unlucky men who were falsely convicted of the Birmingham pub bombings.

He was not even on the fateful trip to James McDade's funeral that resulted in the arrest of the other five. He merely went to Birmingham's New Street station to see them off.

The only reason Hugh Callaghan came to be at New Street in the first place was because he owed Dick McIlkenny a pound and had called round at his house to repay the debt. When he got there he discovered that Dick McIlkenny was packing for a weekend visit to Ireland. Hughie spent the rest of the afternoon playing with Dick's children and then decided to accompany him to New Street and wave him off. The rest is history.

A mild-mannered, nervous man—then in his forties—Hugh Callaghan was one of the most unlikely IRA "bombers" ever to fall into police hands. In *Cruel Fate* he tells simply, with humour and entirely without bitterness, the story of the nightmare that overtook his life. He writes movingly about his impoverished childhood in Belfast, about life in prison and about his triumphant re-entry into the world. He writes, too, about the unswerving loyalty of his lovely wife and daughter, Eileen and Geraldine. It is a measure of Eileen's courage that, although by

i

disposition a shy woman, she even collected signatures for the re-opening of the case on the streets of Birmingham.

Cruel Fate is the story of an ordinary man who has emerged with strength and dignity from an extraordinary ordeal. Hugh Callaghan is an example to us all.

Chris Mullin

1

EARLY YEARS

I was born in 1930, in Butler Street, Ardoyne, a Catholic district of north Belfast. I was the fifth of nine children—six boys and three girls. Infant deaths were common in the thirties among poor people; our family lost two. Charlie, Tom, Patricia (Patsy), Maureen, Dan, Noel and myself survived.

Ardoyne in the thirties was a small place. I knew all the children and every family in my street, and many were related to each other through marriage. Ardoyne was typical, I suppose, of small towns throughout Ireland, although in Belfast there were Catholic districts and Protestant districts. The two communities had quite different cultures, but as a child I did not experience the marked divide that exists today in Belfast. I had many Protestant as well as Catholic friends.

Our lives were dominated by the constant struggle against poverty and unemployment. There were few opportunities for Catholic families, and it was common for the men in the family to be working away from home, in England or America. Few escaped the poverty of unemployment and the struggle to feed large families. Nevertheless I have happy memories of my childhood. It was a simple life, with few material possessions.

I spent my time, like all the Ardoyne children, out playing in the streets, with nothing more than a ball to play with. Playing soccer on the street outside our houses gave the children endless hours of uninterrupted play. Our mothers would give the occasional shout to come indoors at meal time. To be out playing in the street with pals and being fed when we needed it was enough. If we were lucky when we left school we might get a job in the mills as unskilled workers.

In the very early days in Butler Street we lived in one room in a terraced house. Each room was rented to a different family. However, by the time Noel, my youngest brother, was born, in 1939, we were able to rent the whole house.

My father, Patrick, was in the British army most of his life. He fought in the 1914–18 war and later in the Second World War. He was a self-taught man; he read and travelled widely. He could turn his hand to anything; he was always repairing this or that around the house. He was never still. He was a great talker too; he had a lot of stories about his army life and his travels. In the pubs he was always the centre of attention. He could sing a good song and had a powerful voice with a lot of the charm the regulars in pubs liked; it was never quite appreciated in the same way at home among his family.

There was another side to him, however. He was a dominating man, and drank too much; when he came home he was authoritarian and ruled us all with an iron rod—not even my mother escaped. We obeyed and never challenged him. My mother might attempt to if she saw him being particularly harsh, but her efforts were feeble compared with his responses. She would withdraw from him, frightened by his reaction. In his frequent drinking bouts he became violent and lashed out at the children.

He came in once from the pub, and he wanted Tom to play the harmonica—my father had given it to him as a present. Tom told him he had sold it to some lad in exchange for the money to play a game of billiards. My father jumped out of his chair and ordered Tom to get upstairs. We all knew what that meant: Tom was going to get a hiding. A few minutes later I could hear him screaming and pleading for mercy, saying how sorry he was, and then the noise of my father belting him. I went cold with fear. My mother and Patsy were there too, and we just looked at each other. We couldn't help Tom in any way. My mother shouted to my father to leave him alone, but he just ignored her.

At that moment I absolutely hated my father. He was just an overbearing brute and a bully. I could never respect him after that. Once I mitched from school after being out because of ringworm. I was cleared to return to school, but decided to prolong my break. I was caught by the school inspector, who met me in the street and asked why I wasn't at school. I said I was still off sick with the ringworm, but I obviously hadn't convinced him: when he went to check at my house his suspicions were confirmed. Fortunately for me my father had just left the house when the inspector called, otherwise, as my mother said, "you would have got what Tom got." I lived for a long time in dread of getting the same punishment, and spent my time avoiding my father.

That episode sowed the seeds of the revulsion I feel today for violence and brutality, especially that inflicted by the strong on the weak.

My father used to come home at night sometimes with his drinking pals and act the big man, showing off his sons. He would say, "This is my son Hugh. See how straight and upright he stands!" I always walked fast and had a habit of swinging my arms. "Hugh would make a good soldier. He's definitely suitable for the army. They'll make a man of him." He thought a career in the British army was a noble ambition for any young man; he, of course, was a shining example of what the British army could do for a man. (When I was old enough I asked my mother if I could join the navy, but she refused. She needed me at home, she said.) Other times, just to impress his fellow-boozers, he commanded us to sing and entertain them. He drank most of his money, and often we would be without food on the table or shoes to put on our feet. My mother suggested once that his constant repetition of the song "Inniskilling Dragoons" might be changed for another tune. He picked up a little delf doll from the mantelpiece and hit her between the eyes with it. My mother, with young Patsy, ran terrified and bleeding to a neighbour's house. Tom was later sent by my father to fetch Patsy. Still too terrified, she refused to come home. My mother remained with Patsy for another few days till his temper cooled off.

When he was away I borrowed a pair of his army boots—too big for me, of course, but better than nothing; we would hide up in the fields when we knew he was coming home and I would sneak back later and restore them when he wasn't looking.

My mother, Rose, was completely subordinate to him. She rarely stood up for herself, though he treated her so badly and showed so little concern for how she would manage the demands of a houseful of growing children. She was a gentle, patient woman in those days, who never complained.

As a child I always saw my mother with a baby in her arms or waiting for the birth of another. She was very resourceful with the little money my father gave her. In the early days, before any of us started work, she depended totally on my father to provide for us all; with him drinking the way he did, she might be lucky to see the rent. We were always in debt. We lived on a diet of potatoes and margarine, sometimes dried eggs and home-made bread; on very bad days we went without. Life was a constant struggle. It was, of course, a life common to all poor families in Belfast in the 1930s.

I witnessed a child dying on my mother's knee—a baby girl. Another child died a few years later of TB; but infant deaths were so common that families just buried their children and carried on. My mother often looked sad and withdrawn. It's hard to imagine when I look back just how women survived such dreadful suffering.

Maureen was the oldest. During my childhood she went to live with my grandmother because of ill health; my mother thought the country air would be better for her. I don't remember seeing a lot of her. Just occasionally, when I went to the mill with my aunts, I would see her. She dressed very smartly and fashionably, I remember; she was fair-haired, with deep-blue eyes, in stark contrast to myself: I was dark-skinned, with jet-black hair. People in her job remarked on me and were surprised that I was her brother. I remember some talk at home about Maureen wanting to become a nun. If she did, she never made it: she had a very weak heart, was always ailing, and died in her twenties.

At four years of age I used to walk as far as the school doors with Tom and Charlie and then run back home again. One day I decided to follow them all the way. Charlie shouted at me to go home, but seeing all the others going to school I really wanted to join them. I followed in behind children who I thought looked about my age and sat at a desk in the back row, preserved, I later learnt, for "dunces." All the class laughed, drawing the attention of the teacher to my presence. "And what have we here? Who is this young man?" She marched me up to the front of the class, delighted to find a willing pupil at last. "How did you find your way here?" I explained that I had followed the other children. When I told her my age, a ripple of laughter ran through the classroom.

Sadly, I was sent home, but a year later I ran willingly through the already familiar door. On my arrival the headmaster, Dan McVeigh, remembered me, and gently promised not to send me home. He asked me if I had brought my books with me; I assured him I had. He asked if I had forgotten anything. No, I hadn't, I replied. "What about the *Irish News*?" "Oh," I said, "I didn't think I was allowed to bring it." I wasn't, of course, but at that age I had started to be aware of the paper and looked at it frequently in our house. It must have reached Dan McVeigh's ears.

School days were happy, purposeful days for me. I liked the activity all around me. As I moved up to higher classes I enjoyed English and history. Books were a scarce commodity, but I would read anything. I frequently brought the *Irish News* to school and had a good read under the desk.

Children from poor homes, which usually meant large families such as ours, were given free school meals. For some reason, school meals could not be obtained at Catholic schools, and we were required to have our daily meal in the local Protestant school. Every day I would go along with a few other children to the Protestant school to receive our best meal of the day. I suppose there was a bit of a stigma attached to us in being singled out like this, but we never noticed it. I looked forward immensely to that meal. We were well cared for and treated with great kindness. The cook would greet us at the door and she'd go out of her way to make sure we had enough to eat. The school caretaker, Alfie Gardner, always welcomed us and ushered us in to "sit down and eat up everything." He used to pat me on the head and ask, "Are you sure you've had enough?" "Yes, sir. Thank you, sir," I would reply, very grateful for a good feed.

Years later I was reading a football book and I recognised Alfie's face. I learnt that he had been a goalkeeper for our local team, Cliftonville, as well as an Ireland goalkeeper. I had great regard for him already, but after that he went up even higher in my estimation!

Our street was at the foot of the steps leading up to the church. From the steps you could see life going on every day of the week. Butler Street was also known as "the Pad." It was a meeting-place, and after Mass on Sunday it wasn't unusual to see children and bigger lads playing soccer, twenty a side. In the winter when the snow had turned to ice you could see all the local youngsters having a slide on the ice from the top of the Pad to the bottom.

Summer brought out the gliders. This was daredevil stuff. As we raced down the hill we never saw the danger of the crossroads where cars would emerge. We often played handball for hours, going home only for a drink and—if we were lucky—a piece of bread and jam. Our street was a buzz of activity and life.

The evenings would bring a change of scene, and sound, to the street. All the big fellas would gather at the corner and, to the residents' delight, start singing. Their orchestra was a mouth organ player. The singing went on for hours in the summer months. When my brothers and I grew up we joined them, and we were regarded as quite good singers. Tom could harmonise to any song better then any singer I have ever heard.

My passions as I grew up were football, the films, and singing. The school encouraged Gaelic football, but I was better at soccer. I couldn't wait till after school to get my little tennis ball and play soccer out in the street. I would play for hours with pals like Paddy Cassidy and John McLoughlin from Chatham Street, and ask for nothing more. I remember one day my headmaster coming up Butler Street and frowning on me. "So this is what you get up to, is it? Playing soccer!" He was not impressed.

When Charlie started work, his small wages made a big difference to our income, but my mother soon became totally dependent on the money; in fact Charlie's wage packet was collected even before he arrived home on pay day. He worked at Kennedy's Mill in the Falls Road. Every Thursday at midday I had to run across town to collect his wages for my mother. It was over a mile and a half away from the school. She couldn't wait till the evening, as often there would be empty cupboards and no milk for the baby.

I frequently got the cane on my return to school for being late. I used to forgo my school dinner, saying I was getting it at home. I would never say why. Everybody has their pride, I suppose. Later on the headmaster called me into his room and revealed that he had found out about this regular Thursday errand. He was very decent about it, and told me I should have explained what I was doing and he would have understood. I was grateful for his concern, but I offered no solution. Thereafter he made a very considerate arrangement for me to have an extra half hour or so every Thursday afternoon.

While I was still at school I worked at weekends as a messenger boy, delivering meat to the big houses. I decided one day that they could all wait while I watched my favourite team, Belfast Celtic, playing in Cliftonville football ground. I perched the butcher's bike against an outside wall, stood on it, watched the whole match, then went on my way to deliver the messages. I was sacked on my return; the customers, it seems, had complained. I didn't give a toss: working on Saturdays denied me precious hours that could have been more happily spent watching football.

I worked another time as a newspaper boy, selling the *Irish News* at the corner of Flax Street. I enjoyed doing that, especially when customers would invite me to keep the change from a threepenny bit. I used to go into the British army barracks after finishing in Flax Street and sell the rest of the papers, and that's where I picked up most tips.

When the war started, everything became scarce, even if you could afford to buy things. There were clothing coupons, but they were often sold to better-off people in exchange for money, which could be used to buy food and other essentials. Clothes were definitely low on the list of priorities.

No-one in Belfast old enough to remember the war will ever forget the Belfast Blitz of Easter 1941. There were three air raids on the city inside four weeks. The biggest one came on Easter Tuesday, when about two hundred German bombers ripped the city asunder. Two hundred people died in that one raid. I was eleven at the time, and for me the experience was terrifying. We were evacuated, and Charlie, Dan, Patsy, Tom, myself and Noel with my mother walked the five miles or so to my grandmother's house in Mossley on the outskirts of Belfast. As we passed some of the streets we saw several houses still burning, with people all around trying to salvage their possessions. There were craters in the roads; everywhere there was destruction, and the people looked shocked and bewildered. Today's pictures of refugees walking along highways fleeing war zones always put me in mind of that time.

We were happy to stay with our grandmother for several weeks. She cared well for my mother and the seven of us. We were, of course, always hungry, made more so by the country air. I frequently raided the pantry at night when my grandmother was asleep. I don't know how she managed it. She used to say she would prefer if we only stayed for a week, but I think she enjoyed having us just the same.

Going to football matches on a Saturday afternoon was what life was all about. With Paddy Cassidy and John McLoughlin, my friends since infant school, I walked to all the big matches. As we went along the streets the little tennis ball would come out and we would dribble the ball back and forth to each other on our journey through Woodvale Park and down the Springfield Road. When we got to the grounds the task of getting a lift over the turnstiles would begin. We would wait and bide our time for an adult to lift us over. Just when you might give up hope of getting a lift a few latecomers would come along and do the Good Samaritan. During midweek matches we might not succeed in getting in at all, and then we would have to wait until half time, when everyone could get in free.

When I completed primary school at the age of fourteen the headmaster tried to persuade my mother to let me carry on to the secondary school in Harding Street. There was no chance. The possibility of another wage packet, however small, was much more important to my mother than any grand ideas Mr McVeigh had about furthering my education. I was not surprised at my mother's response: few lads I knew were destined for secondary school. Besides that, I was grown up now, fourteen years of age! I was keen to be a man and do a man's job.

My father was demobbed in 1941 because of ill health. He came back for a while and made all our lives hell. He had always been an active man; unemployment and having very little money drove him further into the clutches of the pubs. My mother struggled desperately to feed us. She would stand outside the dole office with a child in her arms, another by her knee, waiting to catch my father before the money was lost in the pubs. Women neighbours used to say to Patsy how they pitied my poor mother with a man like him to deal with. Eventually he left for England to find work. Sadly, none of his children missed him greatly. His presence around our home always created anxiety and fear, and as his health deteriorated he became worse. He got a job in England, and for a short while he wrote home and sent my mother some money, but it didn't last long. The letters and the money stopped coming; we never heard from him again. I often saw my mother staring out the window, hoping to see him coming. She missed him, I suppose, even though he was appallingly brutal to her most of their life together. We heard from someone once that he was living in London; but he never came home again.

My family loved to sing. A few years before my father went away for good we had our best times singing together. Many evenings at home we would all just sit down and start up our own little concert, singing in harmony, with one of my brothers on the harmonica. Neighbours called us the "Singing Callaghans," and sometimes invited us into their houses to sing for them on special occasions. On summer nights we would sit out on the corner of the street with our neighbours and sing long into the evening. Favourite songs we might sing over and over again. Moore's melodies were great to harmonise, like "The Last

Rose of Summer" and "Oft in the Stilly Night." I first sang on the stage when I was six years old, at the request of the headmaster. I disappointed him later when I refused to join his choir; it interfered with my football games in the street.

Tom was my hero. He played the pipes. I followed him to all the pipe meetings and shared his love of pipe playing. We even went to hear the bands playing in the Orange Day parade. Tom knew every tune played. He practised his pipes for hours and hours. I really envied him: he could go anywhere and always be welcome with his pipes.

The Twelfth of July was always an eventful time in Belfast. My understanding of the history of it all was limited. To me it was the time for the Protestant people to celebrate, just as we did on St Patrick's Day. For three weeks beforehand the Orange bands would be practising in the streets, marching up and down. The red, white and blue of the Union Jack would be starting to show in shop windows and on of the rooftops of tall buildings. All the factories and work-places were either owned or controlled by unionists, and all the workers had to take their annual week's leave starting on the eleventh of July.

On the big day the drums would become ear-splittingly loud as the bands passed Catholic churches or came close to Catholic districts; but it was quite a spectacle just the same. Despite the undertones, I always enjoyed watching the parades on the Twelfth. However, as the evening drew closer, the celebrations and bonfires would start in earnest. Catholics stayed indoors, or at least stuck to their own districts.

I got my first job in the mills as a general hand. There were few men employed at the mill: hard though the work was, it was seen largely as women's work. They worked barefoot, and the floor was always covered in water and thread. It was a hard, long, physically uncomfortable job, and you had to stand all the time. But it was a job, and better than the dole queue. I left it as soon as I could and got a better job in Young's lemonade factory on the Springfield Road, working in the main with men. I had arrived!

It was, however, a boring, repetitive job, watching bottles spinning round in machines, removing them, and filling crates. We did this for eight hours a day, with a half-hour break at midday. We sat in groups of six, and we used to sing our heads off over the din, just to relieve the boredom. We had good crack, talking endlessly about football, local affairs, the latest films, girls—everything that made up our lives at that time. Boring though the job was, the company of the other men and the good humour made it tolerable, and it was never very long to pay day and the weekends.

Money was hard earned. If you lost a shilling or two it could set you back for weeks. I remember once changing jobs and going back later in the week to collect my holiday money, which would have been a lot for me in those days: £2 5s. I went to the bookie's and spent the five bob and discovered to my horror that I had lost the remaining two pounds. I couldn't believe it—my whole year's holiday money! Every inch of ground in the factory was searched over and over again, but to no avail. To drown my sorrows on the way home I went for a pint, and, still desperate about my great loss, decided to take one look in the bookie's. I retraced my steps to the spot where I had placed my bet, looked down, and in disbelief saw my wage packet lying on top of a pile of betting slips. What a relief! It was a million-to-one chance.

In my early teens I played for a local soccer team called Barnsville, which was part of the Confraternity League. They were not the best side, but they were a great bunch of lads. I was at my happiest in those days, and playing football was my consuming passion. I would love above all else to have been able to play football professionally. I was good, but not good enough. There were things on my mind that distracted me, not least the difficulties at home. Father Joseph, who organised the team, used to say, "You'd be a very good footballer, but your mind isn't on your game all the time." I can see him still, standing on the sidelines shouting and cheering on the players, especially the losing side.

I was an ardent supporter of local teams, especially Belfast Celtic. I hardly missed a game. It was an interest that never declined, but as I got older I turned my attention further afield to the English league games. A friend of mine emigrated to Birmingham and used to send me the *Sports Argus*, a football paper, which I read avidly. I knew a lot about the English league, especially the Birmingham teams, before I ever set foot on English soil.

I got the taste of my first pint of stout at sixteen years of age. With friends of the same age I used to go down to pubs near the docks so as not to be observed by disapproving adults. Saturday nights were spent in the local dance hall at Holy Cross. I couldn't dance, but I liked the music and the chance it gave me to meet a girl. My dancing wasn't my best attraction, but with a few drinks inside me it didn't deter me all that much. I wasn't a big drinker but I'd have just enough to put me in good form for the night's entertainment. Just to listen to the music and hear the latest songs from the shows was pleasure enough for me.

Going to the pictures was another favourite activity, and a lot of my weekly wages was spent in the picture-house. In the days before there was a television set in the district, not to mention in everyone's home, the films were a special way of escaping the harshness of life all around. In my day we were spoilt for choice, with three or maybe more cinemas in Ardoyne alone.

We would often go in a gang to the cinema, perhaps pairing off when we got inside. Always in our gang would be Paddy Cassidy and John McLoughlin. On different occasions I would go in a foursome with Jean Beggs and her friend Julia Bermingham and Julia's boy-friend. There was always a special lovers' spot in the cinema where courting couples would go. I often went there with Jean when we started dating regularly. She was great fun and terrific company. We liked the same type of films too. I spent so much time at the pictures that I became an expert on films and film stars. With or without friends I would sometimes see three films in one day, catching the mid-morning, early afternoon and then the evening showing, especially if it was a film I especially liked. Forty years later I still love a good film.

Jean and Julia were best friends, and they looked out for each other. Julia frequently reconciled Jean and me in our many arguments. I believe she still lives in Belfast.

My mother became very despondent after my father deserted her. She went downhill and lost all interest in her home. The house had none of the glow I felt when I went into my friends' houses. My mother sought the company of her sisters more and more, and they would take her for a drink and momentarily lift her spirits up; but there was always the next day to face. She deteriorated rapidly; she started to borrow money, and fell victim to unscrupulous moneylenders.

The pawnshops were a great resource in those days for people who needed money quickly. Every poor family was familiar with them. You never knew what would end up being pawned.

It was terrible to watch her decline in this way, and we all felt it deeply, especially Patsy. My mother in her later years became totally dependent on Patsy, who was just a young woman, not yet twenty. Patsy ran the home and did all the errands. She was wonderful; nothing was ever too much for her, but I don't know how she stuck the responsibility. She was completely selfless, going without any pleasures she could have had so as to take care of my mother. And she had her own difficulties. Her hearing gradually started to go in her early adulthood; I don't suppose she was ever given the medical attention she needed.

We made our lives as best we could, cooking and washing and providing for ourselves. None of us were keen to bring girl-friends or boy-friends home. You wouldn't know what to expect.

Charlie was a different character. Nothing bothered him much, and he troubled no-one. He went to work, came home and cooked a meal, then spruced himself up for the night and went out and enjoyed himself. He was a happy-go-lucky bloke who didn't let things get him down. He did a spell in the RAF. Charlie had a wonderful singing voice and a terrific memory for songs.

With Patsy's help my mother remained protective of my brother Dan, despite her own troubles. Dan remained childlike, unable to mature mentally into adolescence. He was always alone, wandering round the place, unable to communicate with other people. We protected him and ourselves against jokes and ridicule from the outside world. Dan was and remains blissfully unaware of his difference from the rest of us. Patsy cared for him when my mother died, and is still doing it today.

The strain of hiding family secrets and the shame I felt—though I would never admit it—created in me a lasting tendency to be anxious and to fret over everything in my life. I would often dodge Jean's questions about my family. I never wanted her to know the full extent of our problems at home.

I often dreamed of escaping from it all, just as they did in the films. An aunt of mine, my father's sister, came over to Belfast once from America; it was long after my father left. She stayed with my father's family near the docks—my mother wouldn't see her. "I wish your mother would talk to me," she told me. "I'd ask her if I could take you to America with me." Once when I spent an afternoon with her she asked me to give my mother a letter. I knew what was in it, and I was buzzing inside with the possibility; but fate decided otherwise. My mother read it and immediately said, "You're not going to America." She wrote her answer and I gave it to my aunt. My aunt looked sad, gave me a hug, and said, "I could have made you happy." I never heard from her again.

Two years before my father left home I remember Noel, the youngest, being born. The midwife came to the house, and Noel was born in the parlour. The midwife patted my head and said, "You have a new baby brother. Would you like to keep him?"

With Patsy, Charlie, Dan and Noel still at home with my mother, my thoughts began to turn towards emigration. All four of them are still at home today. None of them ever married. I was always on the look-out for a better job, but of course there was little to choose from. Good jobs were scarce, especially for Catholics. Having no prospects for improving my life made me frustrated. What had I to offer any girl? I applied for an engineering job. I waited a week, another week, then the word came that they had no vacancies. I was bitterly disappointed when I was turned down. There was little to hold me there. It was time to pack my bags.

I decided to head for Birmingham. I knew people there, who had often invited me to stay with them. I took up their invitation and left for Birmingham in November 1947, at the tender age of seventeen. I was desperately sad; but I looked forward to a life with better prospects, and J went away determined to make something of myself.

If I had got that job I might have married and settled down in Ardoyne. I believe I might never have left Belfast. My life would have turned out very differently.

2

A New Life in Birmingham

The only time I had ever left Belfast before was to travel to Dublin to see soccer matches, and that was always with a crowd. On this grey November day in 1947 I set out for England on my own. There was nothing unique about it: thousands had done it before me. Later my brother Tom was to emigrate to Birmingham also. When I look back, though, at how innocent and unprepared I was, it makes me smile.

If I was apprehensive about the journey I was saying nothing about it to anyone in my family. They might easily have persuaded me not to go. All our farewells were said, and that was it. The ship to Heysham took hours longer than usual to reach there. Everywhere was fog-bound, and there were long delays at each connection. The clock in New Street station showed 7 p.m. when I arrived in Birmingham holding my one small case in one hand and the instructions on how to get to my friend's home in the other.

Handsworth in 1947 was a middle-class district, with nice houses and well-kept lawns. The streets were clean, and the shops were well stocked. People appeared prosperous; even my friends from Belfast had come a long way. Their house was luxurious compared with what I had left behind. There was a general air of comfort, which I wasn't used to.

There were very few Irish in Handsworth at that time. I found it hard to adjust to life in a big English city. It took ages to get across the city; back in Ardoyne everything was within walking distance. Living with Belfast people, however, helped enormously. They directed me and showed me the ropes.

I got my first job in a factory in the Winson Green area. At seventeen I was very shy, and starting work in a factory in a strange city was a daunting prospect. When I spoke they couldn't understand my accent. I had to repeat myself several times, which caused a lot of embarrassment. They used to think I had a Scottish or north of England accent. But if they thought I was difficult to understand, a cousin of mine who also worked in the factory was worse. He had started to speak with a put-on Birmingham accent. The blokes in the canteen used to ask me what he was talking about!

Birmingham people were used to Irish immigrants, which certainly helped. I found the local people generous, warm, and trusting. I was thrilled when I was asked to join the works football team, and I surprised myself with how well I played. I got great satisfaction in doing what I enjoyed most before I came to England; and playing really brought me out of myself and helped me gain confidence and make friends. The people I worked for and with in Birmingham treated me with kindness and respect.

Factory work was plentiful, although most factory workers depended on overtime for a good wage packet. Being young and single, with lots of strength, I was prepared to work long hours, including weekends and double shifts, sometimes working through the night with an hour's break and starting another shift in the morning. By my previous standards I could earn a very good wage. It gave me my greatest pleasure to be able to afford to buy my young brother Noel his first real football boots and to be able to send Patsy a few bob.

I had read for years about the English soccer league, and I followed it avidly. I had always looked forward to the day when I might be a spectator at an English big league game. The first game I went to was a classic, Aston Villa v. Manchester United. It was a marvellous feeling to stand with seventy thousand other people at a football match. Afterwards the pubs would be buzzing with excitement. People knew each other, and the Irish community in Aston was large and well established. Over the years I became a devoted follower of the fortunes of Aston Villa.

Shortly after I started work, Ireland was playing England at Goodison Park in Liverpool, and I went to see it. When the Irish team came onto the pitch it was pure magic for me. You would have thought the game was being played in Ireland. It was a wonderful feeling. The Scouse accents shouting for Ireland added to the atmosphere.

I developed a great affection for the people of Birmingham. But in spite of the contentment I found in my job and being able to spend some money, being able to go to any football match I wished, I kept saying to myself I wished I had all this back in Belfast. I was homesick, and Birmingham on a Sunday afternoon stuck in digs was a lonely place to be. I missed the friendship of my own kind, and I missed my family.

I kept myself active, but the ache was always there, for better times, happier times, even if I had less money in my pocket. I yearned for my home city; and eventually I went back. I went round to all my old haunts, met old pals, and had a thoroughly good time. I went to the matches with the boys, and did all the things I used to do; but the connection was broken. I knew it was possible for me to go back to Birmingham now and settle down. I suppose I got my homesickness out of my system. Jean in the meantime had got married. I came back determined to settle down and make Birmingham my home.

I moved from Handsworth to Aston, which had a strong Irish community and was altogether more homely and friendly. I eventually started to enjoy life mixing with my own. But the Irish in Aston were far from prosperous. Most lived in digs, usually in run-down houses owned by Irish, Polish or local landlords, who exploited us for all we were worth, which wasn't a lot. Rented rooms in decent houses were difficult to find, especially for Irish people. Notices in windows frequently stated, *Rooms to let—no Irish need apply*. But there were plenty of houses where the whole house would be let to Irish people. I lived in a few places like that, and there was always plenty of company, even if some of the digs were rough and ready.

Sixways, Aston, was where we all met on a Saturday night. I came across lots of people from home, and we would have a drink before going on to a dance. Our favourite haunt was the Exchange pub, which was within walking distance of the dance hall. We would arrive at the Albert Hall for the dance in high spirits. I was a shy person and not forward or pushy; but with a few drinks I could get up enough courage to get up on the floor and ask a girl to dance.

It was at one of these dances that I met Eileen. Eileen comes from near Ballina, County Mayo. She was always with a crowd of girls who were in digs with her; I was friends with all the girls, and I would dance with most of them in the course of the evening. At the weekends we were out every night, and the crack was good; but by Monday our money was spent and we would have to get an advance on our wages. Eileen and I started going out during the week to the pictures or just to the pub. She was good company, and all her friends in the digs thought highly of her. (They have remained lifelong friends.)

We were married in 1956, when we were both in our mid-twenties. The wedding was a modest affair, with a celebration after the church in a room over a pub. In those days families in Ireland couldn't afford to travel over for weddings; but I was content to be married and to have found a nice woman to settle down with. We were given a week off work and we spent it sorting out our new home, one room in a large old house in Birchfield Road, Aston, owned by a Polish woman. The room had very little furniture, just a big old-fashioned bed, two chairs, and a wardrobe. Most of the other tenants were Irish. We shared the toilets, the bathroom and the kitchen with everyone else in the house.

It was difficult to make a home of such a miserable room, but Eileen had the knack. She made it comfortable and warm, and we settled down to married life. Eileen still went out with the girls, and I went with my friends to the pub or on a Saturday to a football match. I continued playing football as well, though too many late nights and hard work with long hours were taking their toll.

One day I got a call from the police at my work-place. Unable to contact me, Tom had rung them with the news of our mother's death. We travelled home as soon as we could for the funeral. We couldn't get a flight, couldn't get a booking on the Liverpool boat, and ended up going from Holyhead and making the long journey up from Dublin to Belfast; and my mother was buried by the time we arrived. Her sister paid for the coffin, and Patsy, Noel, Charlie and Dan were there to bury her. I know the cemetery where my mother was buried, but not the spot where she was laid to rest. It is an unmarked grave. I stayed just a few days with Patsy and then returned to Birmingham. My mother's last years were sad and lonely, and the pain of desertion never got any easier for her.

Geraldine was born in 1958. The first few months in the small room with a baby were difficult. Often I would come home from work and have my tea and go straight out to the pub just to get a bit of space and away from the claustrophobia of the overcrowded room. Eileen was devoted to Geraldine, who flourished in her care. She never complained about lack of sleep or the difficulties of being cooped up in one room with a growing baby. It was undoubtedly stressful for me in such overcrowded conditions. We needed more space. I began to develop stomach problems, brought about by anxiety, my doctor said.

We applied to be rehoused by the local authority, but it took a long time, because we had only one child: in those days people with three and more children were sharing one room. We were finally rehoused in a small two-bedroomed terrace house. It was a very welcome break, and the quality of our lives improved greatly.

Geraldine was an only child, quiet but confident. She made friends easily, and there were always children in and out of the house. She was good at school, and we always got good reports about her. We went out together—nothing very exciting; when she got older we went to the pictures together. She was a typical Birmingham girl, although, because we were Irish, her Birmingham accent was slightly modified. She gave us very few problems, though she knew her own mind and was ambitious and wanted a good education.

Eileen and I lived a very ordinary, quiet life in Birmingham. Eileen had her circle of friends, and they went to bingo or to each other's houses, visiting and talking. Geraldine and Eileen frequently spent summer holidays in Castlebar. I liked going to the dog track and having a little gamble. I liked to see Aston Villa play at home, and to go to the pub for a drink after the match. I had no particular interest in politics, though as working-class people we saw ourselves as natural Labour voters.

In the early 1960s work was easy to find. I had several jobs over the years, mostly in factories as a general labourer. I worked all over Birmingham, and I came to know the city well. The people were easy to get along with, and I regarded Birmingham as my second home. But I retained a consuming interest in news about my home city, even though I went home less and less. If I went to Ireland at all it was to Eileen's home in Mayo, and even that we didn't do very often.

Patsy wrote regularly and told me all the news, and she sent me the *Irish News*, and I kept in touch with the football and other events around Ardoyne. When the civil rights marches began in 1968 Patsy wrote and told me about it. Civil rights marchers were being assaulted regularly by the B Specials and Orange gangs. Like everybody else with families in Belfast or Derry, I was worried about them. Catholic districts were taking a hammering every night; I saw in the papers and on television Catholic homes being attacked and families forced to flee. Rows of houses were being boarded up, their owners having fled to the Republic. I constantly expected a knock on my door in Birmingham with bad news.

In 1972 I decided to pay a quick visit to Belfast. I was anxious to see my family and know they were safe. But I picked the worst weekend of all to go, and I got trapped and couldn't get out of the city for a week. I left Eileen and Geraldine in Castlebar on the Friday, promising to be back by the Sunday evening. When I arrived one of the first things I noticed was that all the houses in the street were boarded up. I suggested to Patsy that I would fix the house for her, and she went down and got the timber for me. Patsy, Charlie and Noel all expressed a fear of an attack that night. This dominated my homecoming, and after being away for so long the talk of burning-outs and sectarian conflicts brought home to me in a very stark way that I was indeed back home in Belfast.

I had no desire to stay in, and I wanted a drink. I asked Noel to come out with me down the Falls Road to visit the father of a friend of mine, Tommy Mullin. Noel warned me that it was dangerous, but we went anyway, and on our way I got a few scares. There were several groups of loyalist youths milling around street corners just waiting for bait—any Catholics would do. When I saw Tommy's father he couldn't believe that we had made the journey across. "You'd best get back and stay in your own district. It's not safe here." Another family offered to put us up and advised against going back to Ardoyne. We chewed it over in the pub, but Noel was adamant that Patsy would be worried if we didn't return. As we sat there, several bluish flashes lit up the sky: petrol bombs were being hurled into the Falls by loyalist youths looking for trouble. We decided in the end not to take up our friends' offer of a bed for the night—and it's a good job we didn't. That house and almost every house in Bombay Street was petrol-bombed, and several burnt to the ground. We might not have lived to tell the tale.

By the time we got back, diving and ducking from menacing gangs and the B Specials all the way, Patsy was beside herself with worry. "Where the hell have ye been? The Specials are everywhere; we're surrounded."

It was a long night. The Specials marched up and down the street foul-mouthing people in their homes. Four petrol bombs were thrown in our window, but we managed to put them out. None of us slept a wink; we got out the whiskey bottle and sat out the night, too scared to move. The others in a way had got used to this atmosphere, but I found it shocking and terrifying. Living in Birmingham all those years, I had missed the worst elements of everyday life for Catholic families in Belfast.

That day all the women and children were taken out of their homes and stayed together in a church hall, and then were taken to west Belfast, where they were safer. Patsy went with them. After they had all gone the area was deserted. I was very apprehensive about the whole situation. The expectation that our area would be burnt out was heightened after what happened the previous night in Bombay Street. I had no desire to sit it out and wait.

I asked Charlie what he was going to do, and, as ever, Charlie did his own thing. He took off, and we didn't see him again that evening. Noel and I walked up towards the area where Patsy now lives. There were open fields all around, and we contemplated stopping there for the night. Then we met two friends from Eskdale Gardens in the Glenards estate. We went to their house, glad to have somewhere to go. They were lovely people, very hospitable, and we drank tea and chatted for several hours. We asked if we could stay, and they agreed.

There was a lot of activity outside that night. People kept coming and going, telling us what was happening. Buses were being commandeered and barricades were being built to fight off attacks. We were asked if we would join some others and man a bus that was being used as a barricade in Etna Drive at the entrance to the estate. Noel was apprehensive, and I wasn't too hot myself, but nevertheless I went. We had nothing to defend ourselves with in the event of an attack, which was as likely to come from the B Specials as from Orange gangs—no arms, no petrol bombs; just each other. We spent a good few hours sitting on the bus, and we had a good laugh at the same time. We all needed to see that night through, and at the finish I was glad I stayed on the bus. It helped pass what could have been a long night. It was impressive to see how the Ardoyne people stood up for themselves and their families; I felt a sense of pride and got a great lift out of being part of their efforts to defend themselves, small though my part was.

Eileen would be wondering where the hell I had been all week. It took me another four days before a good friend of our family who worked in Dublin and who was taking his mother and a disabled relative to safety was able to give me a lift to Dublin. Many families were fleeing the city and going south. I was by now flat broke and couldn't offer anything towards the petrol, but my friend was very understanding. When I got to Dublin my friends made contact with Eileen through the Gardaí. They called round to her house in Mayo and gave her a bizarre story, frightening the life out of her. She believed we had been burnt out and that I was injured in hospital in Dublin.

When I finally got back to England the next day I couldn't talk, and the guys in the pub remarked on how quiet I was. I told them I was still in a state of shock after being caught up in the troubles back home in Belfast. I remained in this state for weeks. I kept thinking about Patsy and the others; I had to get them out of Belfast. For months I expected news that they were burnt out or, worse, had been seriously injured in some way.

Back at work I couldn't concentrate on the job: my mind was on my family and their safety. I had developed a duodenal ulcer and started to lose a lot of time off work. Then I was laid off, and I found it very difficult to get back into employment; if you had a bad sickness record, employers wouldn't take you on. Odd jobs were still relatively easy to find through contacts in the Irish pub world. Subcontractors were always looking for labourers who would work for a day here and there. The pay was half what it might be if you were working regularly for them; still, blokes who were laid off like me were always glad to earn a few bob this way.

Eileen was working as a schools dinner attendant, and Geraldine started work as a clerk in the city in the summer of 1974. During the day if I wasn't working—which I hadn't been officially for three years—I would go out to various clubs and pubs and while away the time while Eileen was at work. I collected my social security money once a week, which helped a little with the housekeeping. We hadn't a lot, but Geraldine wanted for nothing—we made sure of that. When she started her first job we were both very proud of her. It was a good job and she could make a career for herself. She was just sixteen, yet she was very mature and responsible.

In the working-class pubs and clubs I would often run into people from home or people whose families I knew. It is in this context that I knew five men whose lives were to be inextricably linked to my own for the next sixteen years. None of them were more than what could be called acquaintances who I had the pleasure of having a drink with from time to time.

In 1974 I had known Billy Power for about five years. We were not particularly friendly; he was younger than me, with a different circle of friends. We met occasionally at the Crossways pub, where we both drank.

I met Gerry Hunter more regularly than Billy. He drank in the Kingstanding ex-servicemen's club, where I would see him once a fortnight or so. We were not close friends, but we occasionally shared a drink with mutual friends.

Johnny Walker I was casually acquainted with. We met at the Crossways or the Kingstanding. I borrowed money a few times from the tote money raffles he ran.

Richard McIlkenny I met in the same places as the others. His wife, Kate, had been to school with Patsy.

I only came to know Paddy Hill in 1974. He drank in the Crossways, and I saw him there or in Lozell's club every other week, and occasionally might have a game of snooker with him.

None of them were close friends of mine, though coming from Belfast (or Derry, in Johnny's case) we would have felt a natural affinity, as any people from the same districts at home would. We were just typical Irish emigrants who on a fateful day in November 1974 happened to be in the wrong place at the wrong time.

3

ARREST

The twenty-first of November was Eileen's birthday, although, for the first time as far as I know, I didn't remember it. The day began routinely enough. Geraldine went off to her job; later in the morning Eileen went to her job in the local school. She and I had arranged to meet later in the morning so that I could give her some money—a promise I regret not keeping. We met at about 11.15 and spent a brief time together; I had the money when we met, but somehow it stayed in my pocket. I headed for the Crossways pub.

Going out that afternoon I knew there was going to be a lot of activity round the Irish pubs all over Birmingham. The body of a young Belfast man, Jamesie McDade, who had blown himself up outside Coventry telephone exchange, was being flown to Ireland for his funeral in Belfast. Eileen and I knew of McDade: he was a well-known entertainer and singer in the pubs and clubs, and I had known older members of his family back in Ardoyne. However, I had no idea he was involved in anything political, and we were completely surprised when we read about his death.

McDade's death was the main topic of conversation within

the Irish community. His body was to be flown out from Coventry Airport that day, and people from Belfast and other parts of the North had made various arrangements to travel to the funeral. I met Billy Power and Gerry Hunter just outside the Crossways; they were going to Belfast if they could raise the fare. Someone in the pub said there was a coach being laid on to Coventry.

Coming from north Belfast, the same area as Jamesie McDade, Billy and Gerry would have gone to pay their respects and combine the trip with a visit to their families. They were also McDade's contemporaries at school, and their wives were friendly with each other in Birmingham. Going to the funeral would have been natural for any of us; I might have gone myself if I had been working. Attending funerals of neighbours, friends and relatives was part of our tradition and culture at home: there is a social obligation to attend. The manner of a person's death or the life they led are not the main consideration. And funerals were in themselves social occasions, where people would meet after a long time. Irish people don't see funerals as something to be avoided.

It was a day for bumping into people. There was an air of expectancy that Jamesie's departure from Coventry wasn't going to be a quiet affair. The police were gathering at the airport and at the place his body was being held. In the Crossways I was talking to a few Irish fellows about McDade when I ran into Dick McIlkenny and Johnny Walker. When they came in, a few minutes apart, we greeted one another, but I didn't join their company. I told Dick I would be around to his house later to repay some money I owed him.

I must confess I didn't have a very purposeful day. I spent a lot of it in the pub and just hanging around; meeting people and having a drink was a way of passing the time. Later in the day I called around to Dick's house to return the money I owed him. He was getting ready to travel to Belfast, and I spent a bit of time with Kate and the children.

I went with Dick to John Walker's house—my first time there—where I met his wife, Teresa, briefly and for the first time. The three of us left together. I had intended at that time to make my way home, but I changed my mind and said I would go to the station with them. We called to Gerry Hunter's house along the way and headed for New Street Station. Billy was already there when we arrived. They had just missed the 6.55 to Heysham, so we adjourned to the bar and waited for the next train, due to leave at 7.55. My suggestion that we go to the Mulberry Bush pub nearby, where the drink was cheaper, wasn't taken up: they didn't want to miss another train.

Gerry went off to phone home to tell them of his coming. Someone commented that a man was watching us. There was a lot of police activity that day, and their observing some noisy Irishmen in a bar wouldn't have come as much of a surprise to us. We joked among ourselves that it might be the Special Branch, but nobody was serious. What would they want from the likes of us?

We spent the time drinking and chatting until the train was due. Paddy Hill arrived at the last minute, all smiles. He had got a loan from a nun in return for painting work when he came back. He was too late for a pint, so he took a sip of someone else's. I got a platform ticket and went with them as far as the train. They were in great form.

On discovering, much to my annoyance, that my unfinished pint had been removed, I left the station bar. I walked passed the Mulberry Bush; I was going to go in for a drink but decided at the last minute to go to Yates's wine bar, which was near my bus stop. There I met an old friend I hadn't seen for ages, John Fannon.

Within an hour of the five men's departure two bombs exploded in the Mulberry Bush and the Tavern in the Town, not a mile from New Street Station. The first I knew was that the light went out in the bar, and it was announced that there was a bomb scare. I went out of the bar, across Cannon Street, and into the Windsor pub nearby, with my drink still in my hand. John was still with me; and about ten minutes later a policeman barged in and said something not very audible about bombs, and advised us to leave.

John and I moved up closer to where there was a lot of commotion going on, quickly decided that it wasn't safe to hang around, and went our separate ways. I spent the remainder of the evening in two other pubs on my route home, and arrived in just after closing time. Eileen was livid. "Where have you been all day? You could have been killed for all I knew. Why didn't you come home? I've been worried sick about you!" She continued to complain about me, and even though I was in the wrong I foolishly argued the toss. I tried to explain to Eileen what a narrow escape I had from being caught up in the Mulberry Bush explosion, which was definitely true of all six of us. We could just as easily have gone there.

I learnt that Eileen had spent most of the evening alone. Geraldine was out with friends. We had no phone, and Eileen went to a call box up the road to track down Geraldine at her friend's house. She had no idea where to begin looking for me. Geraldine arrived just before me, safe and sound. Eileen and I had more sharp words before we went to bed. I was in the doghouse, and the sofa was very uncomfortable. I couldn't sleep thinking about the explosions. I was convinced that I had had a near miss when deciding not to go to the Mulberry Bush, which now lay in ruins.

The house was empty and quiet when I awoke the following morning. Eileen and Geraldine were already gone, leaving me sleeping. News on the radio was dominated by the explosions. It was much worse than I had imagined: twenty-one young people were killed, and over a hundred severely injured. Who the hell would do such an evil thing? Who could plant explosives in packed pubs? Like every other person in Birmingham that morning, I was shocked and dumbfounded. Geraldine was a young girl just like many who lay dead now. She might well have been one of the victims.

The news got worse. Politicians were expressing outrage, and there were reports of demonstrations in Birmingham against Irish people. Factory workers were walking out, and there was talk of repatriation of the Irish. Others were saying this must surely be a hanging offence, although the death penalty no longer existed in England.

Later bulletins announced that five men were being held for questioning. They were Irish, but no names were given. I cannot remember exactly when the police announced that they were looking for a sixth man, said to be still "at large" in Birmingham; I do remember thinking that they were quick, and that the people of Birmingham would be pleased if those who did this thing were caught.

I decided to call on Gerry Hunter's wife, to tell her Gerry was okay, that he had got the train to Heysham on his way to Belfast. I left the house that morning aware that it wasn't the best day to be an Irish person in Birmingham.

Sandra was a Brummie and a very warm, friendly person. I

knew the minute I saw her that something was up. Her eyes were red and she was shaking and agitated. "I thought you were in Belfast," she said to me. "No," I said, "I didn't go. I just went as far as the station." "The police have been here. They've arrested all of them. Something to do with those bombs last night." I couldn't believe it. For a second I thought she must have been mistaken. After all, I had seen them leave Birmingham on a train. She urged me to go, because the police were expected back.

Walking away from Sandra's house I felt a cold sweat come over me. These men were with me! I saw four of them during the day as well. How could they have been involved? It was obviously a mistake. I had to tell someone. It dawned on me that if they found out I was with them I would be picked up as well. I didn't know what to do. I began to quicken my pace. I felt really panicky. I hoped nobody in the street would notice me.

I tried to persuade myself to act normally. I had done nothing, committed no crime. Why should I be so afraid? I spent the rest of the day in a daze, and I kept looking out for any of the men. I felt sure they would eventually be let go. I decided that if they were still being held by the following day I would go and see a solicitor—though with no money and no knowledge of solicitors I had no idea how I would go about it.

I went from pub to pub looking for some comfort, but the talk was all of the explosions. The mood was angry, and I heard a lot of hostile remarks about Irish people. I met a friend, Charlie Sloane, and we went for a drink in a pub where I was well known, but our accents attracted hostile glares, and we left. I met another Irishman who had walked out of his job: he couldn't take his workmates' insults.

Again I stayed out all day. At closing time I made my way home, and as I got nearer to my turning I had an uneasy feeling that I was being watched or followed. I knew every inch of Stanwell Grove, and yet it all seemed unfamiliar. Of course I had had a fretful day, and right then I had had one drink too many. But by the time I reached the house my stomach was knotted with fear.

I didn't get time to turn the key. The door was opened for me; a man's hand grabbed me by the lapels of my coat, pushed me up against the wall, and put a gun to my temple, while a voice shouted, "Don't move!" I could hardly speak with fright. "I've done nothing. I've done nothing." More men crowded round me. They were all in plain clothes—three of them altogether. Eileen screamed for them to leave me alone. She tried to reach me, but they stood between us. I reached out my hand to Geraldine, but I couldn't see her face.

My legs were like jelly, and my whole body shook with fear. The men were violently angry, and started to shove me towards the door. I found myself pushed into the back of a car. The gun was still visible. "Get in and don't move," I was told. They drove like maniacs to Queen's Road police station.

Unknown to me, a few hours before my arrest our home had been taken over by the Special Branch. Eileen's own nightmare started when she arrived home from work that evening. She let herself in the front door, and as she did the sitting-room door opened and a man caught her by the arm. It was getting dark, but she could see clearly that there were people in the room. They asked her where I was, and told her what to do. "When your husband comes in, act normal. Put on the lights, draw the curtains, put on the television—act normal." Shaking with fright, she asked what it was about. There were no replies; they just repeated their instructions.

Eileen had no idea why I should have been picked up or suspected. She could not figure out what it could be about. At the back of her mind she remotely thought it might be to do with the controversy about McDade's death. Lots of ordinary Irish people living in Birmingham and Coventry were being questioned. The police were at the house for some time before Eileen realised that they were after me in connection with the explosions in the two pubs. She was dumbfounded.

Eventually Geraldine came into the room. She was stunned. Eileen urged them to take it easy and not upset her. "Geraldine thinks a lot of her dad. Don't frighten her."

A family friend, the late Tommy Mullin, knocked on our door, and Geraldine, thinking it was me, let out a scream. Tommy had sufficient time to stick his head in and comment wryly, "I see you have plenty of company tonight." He was carted off to the station, but let go a few hours later; alas, that was not to be my fate. Geraldine's scream unnerved the police, and they turned on her. "Any more outbursts like that, young lady, and someone is going to get hurt!"

At eight o'clock or thereabouts a man the others addressed as "chief" came in. He read out a list of names—John Francis Walker, Noel Richard McIlkenny, William Power, Gerard Hunter, and Patrick Joseph Hill—and asked Eileen if she recognised or knew any of them. It took her a while to identify names put so formally; however, the name McIlkenny rang a bell, and she thought Gerard Hunter must be Gerry, whom she knew slightly. The "chief" left, saying little.

When I finally arrived, Eileen and Geraldine were in tatters, their faces red with tears. The manner of my arrest was barbaric, and a traumatic experience for both of them. After I was taken away, Eileen and Geraldine were left with two policemen, who decided to search the house, although they didn't appear to have much of a clue what they were looking for. The police changed shifts during the night, and Eileen and Geraldine were never left alone. They eventually collapsed into bed together, crying inconsolably.

The police left around three o'clock the following afternoon. They had not given Eileen any idea where I was, despite the "chief's" promise the night before that she would be given a phone number to establish my whereabouts. Too upset and too fearful to remain alone, they went to stay with friends that night. By the close of Saturday, Eileen still had no idea where I was.

4

INTERROGATION AND CONFESSION

A s soon as we arrived at the station one of the policemen picked up a phone from the reception desk. He was so excited he was panting. "We've got him! We've got Callaghan!" He gave the thumbs-up sign to policemen who passed him; I heard him mention something about "the sixth one." I said to myself, Christ, they can't be serious! Me! I couldn't believe it.

I was brought into a small, brightly lit interviewing room with just a table and some chairs. It smelt of smoke and bad air, and it was freezing cold. I was given a cup of foul-smelling coffee, which I couldn't drink. It was supposed to sober me up; but the shock I got when they carted me off was enough.

The two officers identified themselves—both of them were detectives, one a sergeant, the second a constable. "We want to talk to you." There were few formalities. I replied to questions about my identity, where I lived, my age, and my place of work. Beyond this I was told little of what I was to expect. I was full of apprehension. What on earth was going to happen to me? I didn't even know if I was formally arrested. The word "arrested" wasn't used; I don't remember being cautioned either. One of them took control and asked all the questions. He fired them at me rapidly and threateningly; he shouted and verbally abused me and my family, making the customary derogatory remarks about Irish people. He started to shout at me about people being blown up with bombs. I said I had nothing to do with bombs. I wouldn't recognise an explosive device if I was shown one.

I was totally confused and frightened. I was still dumbfounded at the very idea of being taken in for questioning about any crime, never mind such a dreadful one as this. My denials were strenuous, but I could hear my voice faltering. Why would I want to blow up Birmingham people? I was a family man living and settled in Birmingham since 1947. I had a sixteen-year-old daughter, a Birmingham girl like any other. The very thought of planting a bomb in a pub that could take the life of a young person just like her, or of any person, revolted me. I told them over and over again where I was, and who I was with, but they refused to believe me. I was slapped across the face. "Don't give us that shit, Callaghan. You were there and you're going to tell all about it."

I was asked about my movements on the evening of the twenty-first. I told them I went to New Street station to see off five people from home who were going to Belfast; that I went for a drink in a nearby pub, Yates's Wine Lodge, and met a friend I hadn't seen for a long time, John Fannon; and that the police came in to tell us there had been explosions in nearby pubs. That, I said, was all I knew about the bombs. I was able to give plenty of details, with witnesses who could verify my movements during the day and in the evening.

They had the names of the five men I left at the station. I was asked for details about them. At that stage I didn't know for certain that they had been arrested, though I guessed by now that they probably were. None of them were people I regularly met, I explained. I couldn't give them one complete address: I knew the street or the district but not the number of their houses. I was older by ten years or more than Billy Power, Gerry Hunter, and Paddy Hill. But my lack of information only added to their suspicions.

I was asked how I knew Jamesie McDade. I explained that he was a well-known singer and entertainer in the Irish pubs, and that I had grown up with older members of his family in Ardoyne. I was initially afraid to tell them about the men going home to his funeral: I knew they would never understand that people would travel to another country just for the funeral of a friend or neighbour, and was afraid that any reference to McDade under these circumstances would just make matters worse for me and the others. However, I did tell them in the end that they had gone to Belfast for the funeral, and that it would be combined with visits to their families. I knew the minute I said it that these people didn't understand. "Gone to bury their IRA man, are they?" I explained again that they also knew him from home; he was a former schoolmate and a neighbour. They weren't interested. One of the detectives started to shout louder and came up close to my face. "You're a fucking liar!"

More questions followed. A lot of accusations were thrown at me about myself and the other five being in the IRA. They suggested I knew a lot more than I was prepared to admit. They were "going to get the truth" from me, however long it took. I wanted to scream. I felt helpless. We were not in the IRA; I knew nothing about the bombs. I heard myself repeating the same words over and over again.

Throughout the whole process neither of them appeared to

be taking notes. I wouldn't have minded, since I had nothing to hide. They never really seemed to be listening to my answers. My shocked reactions to much of what they were suggesting, and my emphatic denials, didn't impress them one bit. It appeared to me that their minds were already made up. They kept interrupting me; one question rolled into another, giving me no time to reply. I sensed they were trying to confuse me, to make me contradict myself. Everything I said was twisted around, and they kept calling me a liar, at one point suggesting that I could have killed my own daughter. I couldn't believe what I was hearing.

The officer who led the interview raised his voice louder and louder, banging his fist on the table. I think he got a kick out of seeing me terrified out of my wits by him and his aggression. He sneered at me and seemed to detest my fear. I hated violent behaviour. Even in these circumstances I found it difficult to shout back. It wasn't in me.

There was never a moment to think or to compose myself. I felt it was all part of their plan to psychologically undermine my certainty about my own innocence. The same accusations were repeated over and over. My head was thumping and my whole body was sweating; I was trembling all over, and I just wanted to escape. I needed sleep. It was all becoming a bad dream.

At some point a sheet of paper was flung down in front of me. "You're involved in all this. It says so here in Billy Power's statement. Read it." I wasn't up to reading anything. The piece of paper could have been blank. "I don't care what that says. It's not true. None of us had anything to do with those bombings." As they had already obtained one confession, implicating me up to the hilt, they told me, it was all straightforward: I should now make a statement, sign a confession. "I'm not signing anything. I had nothing to do with bombs," I shouted. I was becoming hysterical. Both looked very angry and frustrated. They appeared for a while to be getting nowhere.

After a few hours of sheer terror, they eventually informed me that I was being moved to another station. I was hoping they would allow me some sleep first, but I was out of luck. In the small hours of Saturday morning I was taken to Sutton Coldfield, and I was placed in a cell underneath the station. "A fucking pigsty is too good for you," a policeman shouted in from the desk outside my cell.

The cell door was left open. The only furniture was a bed, which I was not allowed to lie on. I was instructed to stand upright. If they saw me close my eyes they would shout in at me, "No sleeping!" I tried a few times to sit on the bed; each time I did someone would yell, "What are you doing? Get up!" The last time I had slept was Thursday night, and this was now early Saturday morning. Outside the cell were two armed policemen. One of them kept clicking his gun and pretending to aim it in my direction. The second one was a dog handler. The Alsatian wandered in and out of the cell, and he encouraged it to come close to me, sniffing and growling. I was afraid to move. They warned me that if I moved or closed my eyes the dog would attack. Throughout my life I was always very frightened of Alsatian dogs. I knew I was being psychologically and physically terrorised. My heart was pounding with fear.

Standing there in the cell, the time seemed interminable. Every once in a while a policeman would look in and shout out some more abuse at me.

Around eleven o'clock on Saturday morning I was called

back briefly by the same officers who interrogated me the night before. I felt like a compliant zombie, subdued, frightened, confused, and by now very very tired. I kept wishing for sleep and a nice cold drink. I was taken to be swabbed by a forensic scientist whose name, I later found out, was Lloyd. My hands were shaking; they felt sweaty and were unwashed. He never looked at me during the whole process and did not speak to me or anyone else. He conducted the business efficiently, from what I was able to observe. I hoped he was an honest man.

I was then returned to the interviewing room to be confronted by my interrogators again. I told them I had a duodenal ulcer, which I half hoped would make them go a bit easy on me. I sat opposite one of the officers at a table answering routine questions about my age and address that I had already answered several hours before. He kept kicking me hard on the shins. The pain was excruciating. Every time I flinched he kicked me again. I couldn't say any more. If I spoke I would be kicked, and if I remained silent I would be kicked. One thing I knew and that was that I wouldn't dare to complain. It was a terrifying half an hour before they left me and I was returned to my cell.

Back again to the interviewing room, this time with a fresh team of detectives. There were three or four men there. I quickly gathered by their attitude and the expression on their faces that this was the "heavy mob," sent in to finish the job. This was no simple case of rough treatment and then being let go: these people were trying to pin something very serious on me and the other five men. I knew too that I would not be able to take much from them. Their very presence terrified me. But Christ, I was innocent, and I would keep saying it!

By now I desperately needed time to myself. I was losing control; I was losing my resolve not to admit anything. A few more hours with these men and I felt I would give up. I asked for something to eat; they said the canteen was closed. I was sick and weak from lack of sleep, food, and drink. I was told to strip, and I was left naked for several minutes; then I was told to dress again, and strip again. The humiliation was unbearable; I have always been a private person. My embarrassment amused all of them, who stood looking and laughing contemptuously.

Three or four men circled me while I remained sitting on a chair. Sometimes they didn't speak, just circled round my back, coming up close to me, breathing on my face and hissing and whispering vile threats and abuse into my ears. Then they would suddenly shout and make me jump. My stomach was churning, and I was crying. When I was at my weakest they whipped the chair from under me.

When I had still just a blanket around me and was feeling very vulnerable and exposed, one of them raised his fist to me. "You will make a fucking statement or we will bash you around this cell." I begged him not to hit me. I pleaded with him to believe my story, which I kept saying I could prove. He wasn't interested; the only thing that was going to satisfy him was a confession. I asked for a drink—I couldn't eat now. My mouth was parched. I could hardly speak above a whisper. Eventually they let me go to the toilet, and I scooped up water in my hands from the sink.

At some point an exasperated officer grabbed me bodily and pinned me against the wall. Strange, animal-like noises emanated from him; his eyes were wild, like a man about to kill. My head hit the wall and bounced back. I was dizzy; I thought I was going to get sick. I really believed he was going to kill me—at least it would have been an escape from this terror.

Another policeman realised that his colleague was going too

far. He pulled him from me, rescuing me like an impartial referee. He put his hand on my shoulder and spoke very quietly. "I'm not like him." He walked me back to the table; I was like a lamb. "Come on, mate, you'll do it for me." I had never experienced such terror or pressure in my life before. I knew before God that neither I nor any of the others had any part in planting bombs. I just couldn't take any more. I begged them once more to believe me, but I just wanted it over with and to be left alone. At my lowest ebb, they seized their opportunity, and I conceded. I agreed to sign a confession.

I was led through the "confession." I hardly spoke or made any contribution to it. I nodded my agreement occasionally about places I was really in and the people I had spoken to; as far as I was aware the rest was a complete fabrication. They suggested names of people who were my accomplices in this evil crime. I offered no details about the explosions—because I couldn't. It was of no consequence to them. My only part in this cruel farce was to put my name to it. I did—knowing it all to be a lie. I was getting them off my back, if only for a while. I convinced myself that as soon as I got to see a solicitor I could deny all this. I would explain the circumstances; I even contemplated complaining about the treatment I received. I now know that this was a very naïve belief indeed.

They read the statement back to me. I wasn't even listening. It was like a bad dream that I would eventually awake from. The statement was placed in front of me. I didn't read it, and in a million years couldn't have read it. At that moment I would have signed anything. With a policeman's hand over mine, "to steady my hand," he said, I signed it in two places. The second section was read back to me, but I wasn't taking it in. It stated, as I learnt later to my cost, that "I have read the above statement and have been told that I can correct, alter or add anything I wish. This statement is true. I have made it of my own free will."

By the time this business was concluded I was totally exhausted and defeated. They all had a smug look of satisfaction on their faces. I wept with despair as the significance of what I had done began to overwhelm me.

The very minute I signed they grabbed the statement and left. I was at last left alone. I had no desire to think or contemplate anything now. I wept continuously.

I was allowed to leave the claustrophobic cell and sit on a bench outside it for a short time. I sat outside with one of the few policemen who were ever to show any compassion or sympathy. I started to pour my heart out to him. He actually listened, which was encouraging. He didn't shout or abuse me.

When I was ordered to return to the cell, I did so feeling emotionally drained. I went over and over the events of the day. I knew I had signed a piece of paper. They said it was a statement made of my own free will; as far as I was concerned I did not sign it of my own free will. Under violence and terror I signed a statement implicating myself and some of the others in a crime we could not possibly have committed. I kept trying to remember what was in it. When they read it to me I wasn't listening. Was it as bad as it seemed? Did it really say we planted bombs in pubs? It was incredible.

That evening and night I alternated between anger and despair. Why were we picked out? Was it simply because we were Irish? I had lived in Birmingham since 1947. It was my home. However, I had failed to convince them of my innocence. I went through elaborate justifications for signing. Who could stand up to that terror? I decided that a good solicitor was my only hope. I resolved that I would ask for a solicitor in the morning. I would tell the solicitor that the statement was a pack of lies, that I was forced to sign it, that everything in it was made up. It all seemed logical and simple. Yet it failed to console me.

I began to imagine all kinds of things. I thought they had arrested Eileen and that she was here in the station. Why couldn't I see her? I suppose I must have lost control. This is what it must be like for people who are going mad. The cold in the cell and my empty stomach prevented me from passing out.

By the small hours of the morning I became more alert, and I was obsessed with one thing. I must be allowed to retract that statement. If it wasn't retracted we could all end up in great trouble. I knew Billy had signed something, and I guessed he did so under the same pressure as I had experienced. I had no idea whether any of the others had signed. I couldn't wait for them to open my cell door. I was bursting to tell them my decision. I actually felt mentally stronger and more determined about my intentions. I had two objectives: to see a solicitor and retract that statement.

I shut my eyes and remained sitting upright on the foot of the bed. When daylight came I was, I thought, ready for them. But it didn't work out as I had planned. I had yet to receive anything to drink. I was dying for a decent cup of tea. I was whisked off in an unmarked car, pushed in the back between two plain-clothes men with two others in front. I recognised one of the officers as the one who had led the interview. I had, of course, no idea where I was going. Sitting in the back between the two policemen I immediately said, "You can't use that statement. It's false. I was forced to sign it, and none of it is true. I was forced to involve Gerry Hunter in something he didn't do." My heart was beating as I spoke. I was petrified, but I hoped I sounded convincing enough.

My remarks drew an instant reaction. The brakes were slammed on, and the policeman sitting in the front passenger seat produced a gun from under his coat. He leaned right over the seat and pointed the gun to my stomach. "You stick to that statement," he said. I didn't stir. I knew he meant business. I was trapped in this car and trapped again by that statement.

The drive to Queen's Road station seemed interminable. Yet it was only a short distance. I knew the area well and it was obvious to me they were taking a long route. They stopped by the lake in Selford Park en route, and one said to the other, "Let's throw the bastard in the lake." I was terrified and didn't move or look in any direction. I knew these men were by now capable of anything. I believed the slightest agitation from me would have made them carry out their threat. Later they drove on to Queen's Road police station. By the time I reached there I didn't know what other evil they might have in store for me. The psychological torture seemed unending and getting worse.

Handcuffed to a radiator back in Queen's Road station, I was questioned again by two very unattractive, sneering detectives, whose comments during the interview showed me how crude and ignorant they were. I again said I didn't want the statement I signed used; I asked for it to be retracted. They just ignored me. "Right then, Callaghan. Who is the head man in your cell? Who is the captain, the brigadier? What about you? Are you a captain?" It was laughable. They asked me about collecting for the IRA, which again I knew nothing about. I learnt later that this referred to John and Richard, who had collected for prisoners' dependants. This money, as far as I knew, went to the families of men in Long Kesh and other prisons in the

North of Ireland.

I remained handcuffed throughout this interview, though I cannot think what danger I could possibly have been. My mouth was dry, my stomach was empty, and I needed a shower. My body and hair were sweaty. I felt foul. I asked for a drink and a biscuit, but, as ever, my request fell on deaf ears.

When the detectives left I still hadn't succeeded in retracting my statement, and now I was told I was going to be charged. The charge was murder.

5

WINSON GREEN PRISON

We received the accusations in silence. To protest our innocence now would be futile—it could even have provoked more assaults. Three days ago we were free men, with few worries. Now we stood accused of this dreadful crime. What was going to happen to us God only knew.

I got a brief glimpse of the other men before we were taken away, my first time to see them since we parted company at New Street Station three nights earlier. They looked dreadful; barely recognisable. Their faces were swollen, with black eyes, cuts, and bruises. Their eyes had a haunted look.

Despite lack of sleep, food and a decent drink I fully realised the significance of the charges. Many times over that weekend I had insisted we didn't do it, but none of those who interrogated me were listening. They were satisfied, the public was satisfied. They were able to wave signed statements in the air, solid evidence of our guilt. The police had it all stitched up. Their job was completed.

Late on Sunday afternoon, two days and two nights after we had been arrested, we were taken by armed police to the central lock-up at Steelhouse Lane, where people are held before being brought before the Magistrates' Court. We couldn't talk on the journey, and we were placed in the police van in such as a way as to make eye contact with each other difficult; yet in the circumstances I was pleased to be surrounded by familiar faces. I felt a sense of comfort from their presence, and I wasn't so afraid. At least I wasn't facing this ordeal alone. I still had high hopes of solicitors getting us out of all this, and I wondered when they would let us see one.

We were handcuffed and shuffled around like dogs while they decided where we should go and what to do with us. Eventually we were placed in separate cells. As on the two previous nights, I was not allowed to sleep. Every now and then throughout the night I could hear screams; I knew someone was getting the treatment. A red light was left on in the cell all night, and the flap was repeatedly opened and shut.

As Monday morning approached I steeled myself against more abuse, and there was plenty of it. As I shuffled around, barely able to move, a policeman put his fist close to my face. "Don't tempt me. Just don't tempt me, you bastard." At some time that morning I was given my first cup of tea. I had to spit it out: it had urine in it.

Early on Monday we had our first meeting with the solicitors, Ian Gold and Anthony Curtis. The encounter with my solicitor, Mr Gold, on whom I had pinned my hopes, was brief, frustrating, and fruitless. We were given just a few minutes to tell all. I had to speak quickly, get it all in. I said emphatically that I didn't want the statement used, that it wasn't true, I was forced to make it. I stated with as much determination as I could muster, "We didn't do this." I wanted to go on about the severity of my treatment, but he seemed in a hurry and was anxious to fill out forms and get all my personal details down. The solicitors needed to complete a legal aid form before they could represent us. I was so frustrated I felt like screaming. Then it was someone else's turn. The entire process took about ten minutes.

I learnt later that Gold was the duty solicitor, who dealt regularly with people held in Steelhouse Lane. He was young, polite, and businesslike; but he appeared cold and indifferent. He gave no opinion or encouragement about our plight. I comforted myself with the possibility that perhaps he would say something when we got to court. Maybe that was how solicitors worked. I had so little knowledge of them.

After the solicitors had completed their formalities we were brought up into a big room and held there for about half an hour before the court appearance. I got a second opportunity to see the others at close range. All of them had cuts and bruises and dried bloodstains on their face and clothes. They looked like death. Our own clothes had been confiscated and replaced with ill-fitting old clothes and what seemed like clogs for shoes. When I looked at the men it was obvious to me that the authorities were deliberately trying to present an image of six ignorant, ill-clad Irish men. We were made to look ridiculous and stupid for our first appearance in court. Later, reports of that first appearance described inevitably our "scruffy appearance." A policeman stood guarding us with a gun in his hand. "No talking, and don't move, any of you, or I'll use this."

The courtroom was packed with officials and policemen of all kinds. I recognised many of them who had put me through it over the past two days. They sat talking to each other with satisfied expressions on their faces, as if they had delivered the goods. I looked out for our solicitors, trying to gauge their attitude, but they were in conversation with court officials; neither of them glanced our way. The whole atmosphere was intimidating. I could almost touch the hatred I felt from all present in the court. The clerks, the magistrates, the press, and the public—there was little difference between any of them as far as I was concerned.

The charges were read out. I was hardly listening. Bail wasn't requested. Gold and Curtis stood up and addressed the magistrates at different times, then sat down. I had absolutely no idea about court proceedings and what role we as the accused played in the whole process. Our solicitors had no time to explain. We were completely ill-prepared. We were like sheep just being led around. "Stand up," "sit down"—we just did as we were instructed by the court officials. I could not actually hear what our solicitors were saying. The court proceedings were such that no attempt was made to include us in any reference to "my lord."

I thought, is that it? Aren't they going to mention our complaints—our injuries? What about the statements? I had told the solicitor I wished to retract the statement; isn't he going to mention that? Then it was all over. I couldn't believe it. What kind of justice was this?

We were remanded in custody to appear later. As we were being brought down, a policeman hinted that a reception committee would be waiting for us at Winson Green Prison, and my legs went like jelly. I heard the term "VIP treatment"—the "red carpet" would be ready for us.

We were shoved into the van to the sound of screaming, jeering crowds. "Hang them! Hang them! Murderers! Murderers!" Maximum attention was drawn to our departure, and for the duration of the short journey to Winson Green, police cars led the way with sirens blaring. They drove at incredible speed, and we were jostled and thrown about, hitting the bars of the traps we were placed in.

The van halted with equal ferocity; I thought I was going to throw up. The Special Branch men in the patrol cars jumped out, panting; they couldn't wait to get at us. "Here they are. Here are the IRA murderers." I was so scared I didn't want to get out of the van. "Come on, you bastard. Out! Run, run!" We were like trapped rats, with nowhere to run except into the trap. A row of policemen stood each side of the entrance; some of them had guns with their fingers on the triggers. The sight and sound of the guns clicking sent the dogs into a frenzy. We were taken out one by one to run the gauntlet. We were hit, punched, and pushed from one to another; their foul language and insults heightened the fear. As we entered this room, booted in with a kick in the small of the back, we were ordered to face the wall. Three faced the wall on one side, three on the other side of the room. They continued to mount surprise punches, thumps and kicks on us while we stood facing the wall. Billy, who stood nearest the door and was getting the worst treatment, put his hands to his forehead to protect himself.

The reception area was packed. Everyone wanted a taste of the action, to unleash their anger, hit out at us. Inmates came to view, encouraged by the staff. We were pushed into a room, and I heard a thud, and another cry from someone in distress. Amid all this chaos we were required to sign for our possessions. As our details were being taken at the desks, prison officers tossed the tables up in the air. "You didn't call me sir. Say yes, sir! Thank you, sir! From now on it's sir! D'you get that?" A table was tossed upside down; I hid under another table in sheer terror and desperation. I just wanted to die. I was soon discovered and dragged out by the hair to line up with the rest. They flung me on the floor at the feet of the other men; I remained where I was. "What's the matter? Can't you get up? Consider yourself lucky you have fucking legs to stand on. Get up!"

We were taken into where the showers were, told to undress and run back again to get our prison clothes, all the time we were being pushed, and kicked around like footballs. Several prisoners took part in this assault. We were taken up a flight of stairs and I remember at the top of the stairs more screws and more prisoners were waiting and baying with excitement ready to attack us. Billy and Dick, just ahead of me, grabbed hold of each other and barged their way through the mob, all the while being beaten and kicked. I followed screaming with pain from a kick I received on my side from the boot of a screw.

We were left in a locked room for a short while. The verbal abuse and threats continued, and there was a promise of more to come. Each of us nursed injuries, our faces covered in blood. My head reeled from pain. My eyes wouldn't focus properly. I began to think we would be better off dead than taking much more of this. We were then dumped in cells, each of us kicked into a cell and the door slammed. We were ordered to stand to attention, face the door of the cell and not to move. Needless to say, we could barely stand up; I could hardly focus my eyes and I kept going dizzy and wanting to pass out. "Move and you will get more, you evil bastard," one of them shouted out when he saw me swaying.

So much happened during those few hours it's hard to relate it in an orderly way. I suppose I only remember the worst aspects of it. We heard them call out, "Send the filthy bastards up." We were dragged one by one to the washroom, like prisoners being dragged to the execution chair. "Move, move, you bastards!" Christ, I thought, this is it! They are going to finish us off. Are they going to drown us? I hope to God they do it quickly! There were flights of stairs. I can't remember if we went up or down, but whichever way it was we ran the gauntlet of vicious, brutal men. By the time I reached the bath the water was red, full of blood and hair from the beaten bodies of some of the others. I was shoved into it; I can't remember if I was clothed or not. On my way out of the bath I fell to the floor; from behind I got another kick, and I fell again at the top of the iron stairs. Dick McIlkenny, who was just ahead of me, caught hold of me. I was convinced we were going to be murdered slowly, the violence of the warders against us was so savage. They behaved like an uncontrolled pack of wild animals. I remain convinced to this day that if that savage assault had gone on any longer, one of us would almost certainly have died. Some of us were already so severely beaten and traumatised that we were too weak to take much more.

I must have passed out, because after the assault—it could have been half an hour or so—I opened my eyes to find a doctor patting my cheeks. I didn't recognise him as a doctor at first, and I curled up, sure I was going to be assaulted again. Then he said, "Come on, come on. You're all right. You've not passed out yet. You're not going to faint on us." He didn't seem anything like a doctor. He nodded to the warder, and I thought he was indicating to him that this bloke can't take any more. However, his own behaviour towards me didn't suggest he cared very much. The screw just bawled at me, "Up you get, and make that fucking bed." I tried, but made a bad job of it. "You must know how to make a fucking bed. Now have it done by the time I get back, or else!" I felt very weak, dying for a drink all the time.

I had a visit from the assistant governor next morning. "Is

everything all right?" I ached from head to toe; every part of my body seemed battered—and he asked me if I was all right! But I was learning fast. Don't complain, I said to myself, unless you want another assault. I mumbled, "Yes, sir." He left.

A few days later I had a visit from a doctor, on the insistence of my solicitor. I wasn't keen to see the doctor; I was afraid the warders would retaliate if I revealed anything about the assault. When asked by the doctor about the various injuries to my ribs, my eyes, and head, I said I fell down the stairs. I regarded everyone who came into contact with me at this time—doctors, warders, solicitors, in fact all officialdom—as my enemies. I drew no distinctions: they were all in this together. For a long time afterwards, every time I closed my eyes the image of brutal men in uniforms and my five friends covered in blood kept coming before me. It was a recurring nightmare.

Thus began my first few hours as a remand prisoner—not yet convicted—in Her Majesty's Prison at Winson Green, Birmingham.

6

ON REMAND

On Tuesday morning we were awakened at dawn. The doors slammed open and screws bawled out their instructions, using the language of the trough. I struggled to lift my body up; I was hardly able to move a muscle. Every part of my body felt bruised, but most of all I ached inside. I couldn't believe what was happening to me. It was like still being alive, yet my body and my mind had descended into Hell.

I followed blindly whatever instructions they shouted at me. Breakfast was thick, cold porridge followed by tea and a bit of bread. It was the first taste of food I had for four days. I ate it.

After our so-called breakfast it was still only around eight o'clock. I wanted to go back to sleep, but the screws wouldn't let us. As far as they were concerned we had had our allotted sleeping time. It was over four nights since I was picked up, and I had hardly had any sleep since then. I desperately needed to close my eyes. During the previous night I had been too terrified to sleep. I was convinced we were due another beating, and as the night wore on my fear was heightened. I must have dozed off eventually, and when they called me in the morning I was surprised I had survived the night.

On our first exercise in the prison yard we had to walk single file, fifteen to twenty paces apart. Screws shouted at us and commanded us to keep moving and not to talk—not that we were up to much by way of conversation. We were surrounded by screws and dogs; there wasn't an awful lot of difference between the two in their demeanour towards us. I remember it being a bitterly cold November day. We were without prison overcoats and we walked around with just pullovers on, but I was really glad to get out. I desperately needed the air and to walk around, to see the sky above me.

Nearly five days of obscene violence and cruelty inflicted on six innocent people by uniformed thugs had taken their toll. We were beaten into submission, worn out and defeated.

The atmosphere in the prison yard was ugly and hostile. Eyes kept appearing at cell windows, and obscenities and verbal abuse were directed at us from all corners of the prison. A bucket was emptied from a cell window right in front of our path. My knees were giving way, and I asked to be returned to my cell. I wanted to walk, but I felt unable to move another step. "Keep moving. We'll tell you when it's time to go in." We kept our heads down and kept going round and round, like dead men on our feet. I was terrified that I would collapse and draw the dogs on me. It was my first walk around a prison yard, and one I will never forget. There was intense hatred and anger in the eyes of the prison officers, believing we were guilty of such an evil crime that tore their city apart.

On Tuesday afternoon Eileen came to visit me, with Geraldine. I was taken from one wing of the prison to another, going up and down endless stairs, passing through workshops full of men all dressed in striped prison shirts. I had no idea the prison was so big. As I passed through these areas I remember saying to myself, Christ, I hope I don't end up like that. It looked a bit like a mental institution. It hadn't yet registered with me that being on remand was just a prelude to permanent settlement in prison, if I was convicted—not a prospect I ever believed possible.

The warders used walkie-talkies as I was escorted from one section of the prison to another. "IRA man Callaghan coming through now." You could see they were just doing it to annoy me and to make sure the other inmates noticed me. When they saw me some of them hissed like cats. "Should be strung up," one of them said. "Animals, that's what they are," remarked another. I didn't respond; I just wanted to keep moving.

Minutes before I was taken into the room for the visit I was instructed to stand to attention by a screw accompanied by a heavily breathing dog. By the time I reached the visiting room I was exasperated. They had achieved their objective: I was in no fit state to meet my distraught wife and daughter.

We sat on either side of a thick glass screen with a square wire mesh running through it. It distorted faces, and voices were muffled. The warders stood close to us, two behind my back, two behind Geraldine, and another one at the door. It was impossible to say or do anything. I could see by Eileen's and Geraldine's expressions that they were shocked by my appearance. I had black eyes, my lips were swollen, and there were cuts on my face, and I had been given an old torn prison shirt to wear. I wasn't a pretty sight.

Geraldine was tearful and looked bewildered by her surroundings. In a way I wished she hadn't come. Eileen was trying both to console Geraldine and to offer what comfort she could to me. She was always strong, but this experience was too much for her. Her eyes were full of tears. I was choked up. Their distress was terrible to witness, and I couldn't even reach out my hand to them.

Eileen spoke in a low voice. The screws ordered her to speak up. She wouldn't, just couldn't raise her voice. I could hardly hear her. There were communicating telephones on each side of the screen, but neither of us could use them. They were cumbersome and impersonal. I put my hand and eyes close to the glass, trying to lip-read what Eileen was saying. She stuck to generalities. "Are you all right? Do you need anything?" "No. I'm okay. We didn't do this. You know that, don't you?" I knew Eileen and Geraldine would not doubt my innocence for a second; I said it for the benefit of the screws, who were all ears. "We're innocent."

The visit lasted ten minutes, before the screw bawled, "Visit over!" I wanted to give Geraldine a hug and reassure her that I was going to be all right. I was instructed to stand to attention. "Ready?" "Yes," I replied. He shouted back at me, "Yes, sir! Say yes, sir!" I did as I was told. I was then marched towards the door, with a screw in front of me and one behind. Just as the door was closing I heard a thud, as if someone had fallen to the floor; I heard Geraldine's cry, "Oh, my dad! Oh, my dad!" I stopped. They ordered me to keep going. Her cry went through me, as if someone had put a knife in my heart. I returned to my cell and wept.

Eileen and Geraldine came back to visit me the next day for another ten minutes. It was every bit as harrowing as the first time; the only difference was that they at least knew what to expect. We were entitled to fifteen-minute visits, reduced to ten minutes if our families wanted to leave clothes or other goods for us. The time to do this was deducted from our visiting time. More time was deducted for searching our visitors as they came in. Our wives were insulted with crude remarks while being body-searched, and had to accept it all for our sakes, knowing that any retaliation might get us into trouble.

Our first few weeks on remand at Winson Green were harsh and cruel. The prison was old, and the cells were damp, cold, and smelly. We spent twenty-three out of every twenty-four hours in our cells. We ate alone, and were isolated from each other and from all other prisoners. We were placed in a disused part of the prison, which had been empty for thirty or forty years, well away from the other prisoners. Specially selected screws were placed in charge of us; they had to ensure above all else that we did not talk to each other. The cells resembled the pictures you would see of prisoners being slung into the dungeons. In the first few days we were prohibited from speaking to each other. If we passed each other going to the showers or collecting our dinners we were watched to make sure we didn't get a chance to communicate. It nearly drove me crazy. To keep my mind alert and prevent me from becoming depressed I would look out my cell window into the exercise yard and watch the men walking round and round the yard. I would focus on one or two and count the times they went round. It was something to do. It helped also to keep a check on time. The end of exercise meant it was dinner-time. I would have contact with the outside world and another human being, albeit a prison officer.

If you are compelled to spend many hours alone and isolated in a confined space with nothing to see or do, your natural inclination is to sleep. But for some inexplicable reason we were not allowed to sleep during the day. If I started dozing off they would bang on the door. "Wake up, you idle bastard!" But what else was there to do? I couldn't sleep at night, not only being fearful of a surprise assault but because it was so damned cold in the cell. I had no desire or inclination to read a paper, write a letter, or do anything with a purpose. I couldn't for the life of me see what harm a sleeping man could do locked up in a prison cell.

"Slopping out" is primitive, crude, and degrading. It made me physically sick. We were escorted even in carrying out this degrading function. We had to slop out one by one to avoid communication—as if any of us would stand to converse holding the contents of our overnight toilet. Though I couldn't express it so at the time, it is the worst example of institutionalised barbarity that human beings are forced to endure every day in British prisons. For some time I was disposing of the contents of my bucket in the wrong place. I got a thump on the back from the warder. "Not in there, mate! In the sluice. Didn't your mates explain it to you?" "How could they?" I said. "I can never see or speak to them." "So you can speak up for yourself after all," the screw commented. He looked surprised. I was too.

The cell window high up on the wall looked out onto the exercise yard. Our cells contained the bare minimum: a bed with one sheet and two striped grey blankets, old and rough; a crude bucket for a toilet; and a plastic bowl and plastic mirror. A razor was issued each morning, when we shaved under supervision. We were allowed radios eventually, and Eileen ordered newspapers for me. About a month after we arrived the furniture and floor covering were upgraded a little.

At night I hardly slept, expecting all the time that the screws would come in the dead of night and do me over again. If I heard footsteps they were definitely coming for me. During the day their demeanour towards us always gave the impression that they hadn't finished with us. A red light was left on in the cell all night long. I got used to it, and came to feel more secure with it on. The spy-hole would be clicked several times a night, and at those moments my fear was at its height.

One night the red light went out suddenly. I jumped up. This is it, I said to myself. I was shaking with fear. I decided to call out that my light was out, then wondered if I had done the right thing. However, it was just the bulb that had gone. I then discovered to my surprise that night duty screws could not gain access to my cell until the morning: they had no keys. I told the others, and relaxed my guard a bit after that.

We had the right as Catholics to attend Mass on Sunday. We were privileged, having our own chapel erected especially for us in a larger cell on our wing. Several screws accompanied us, practically sitting on our laps in the little makeshift chapel. There they sat with their big boots and bunches of jangling keys as if they were guarding animals in a zoo. The priest himself seemed quite unconcerned with the intrusion. I eventually came to see that hour on Sunday as a kind of social gathering for all of us. Sitting there together we had some opportunity to exchange a few words and share a few laughs as well.

Father Masterson was from Mayo and had been a prison chaplain for years. I know that on an individual level he was helpful to some of us, and he had a calming effect in that we were allowed to talk privately to him. On his first visit to me I told him at length that we were innocent, that we were victims of a terrible mistake. He was a kind enough man, listening with great patience; I got the feeling, however, that he had heard it all before. I personally received no solace from his visits: I regarded him as just part of the prison establishment, but I think too that he was afraid to express his opinions. He was a mild-mannered man who probably wouldn't ever assert his opinions to the authorities if it were to create difficulties for him. I was aware, however, that some of the other men found him a great source of comfort, and he helped to calm their nerves. I knew he was limited in what he could do because of the attitude of the prison authorities towards us, but I nevertheless couldn't talk to or confide in him. My talks were always superficial but polite. It has to be remembered that the whole of the media and the public were convinced, even before we came to trial, that we were guilty. Why should he have been any different?

We had to make court appearances regularly, nearly once a week at the beginning. We were called usually hours before we were due to leave. We had to stand by our cell doors and run like hell as soon as our name was called; any delay would result in a torrent of physical and verbal abuse.

The court appearances themselves I often thought were a waste of time. Charges were repeated, our defence would win an extension of time before going to trial, and it was all over usually in a few minutes. Bail was never sought. I couldn't see why they couldn't conduct all this without our presence. We wouldn't have had to make those horrific journeys that took so much out of all of us.

When we got back to the prison our cells were usually changed round and all our possessions interfered with, our letters opened and our solicitors' papers read and often left strewn around. It was harassment of a kind we could do nothing about. Who could you tell without getting a hiding for your trouble? We just had to endure it all. All of it, however, wore my nerves to shreds. It has to be remembered that justice was allegedly taking its course while we were on remand. Under these conditions we were supposed to be preparing for our defence.

I could not begin to concentrate or put my attention on the forthcoming trial. All of us were worn out, exhausted and barely able to get through the day. Yet we were expected, to prepare to defend ourselves against grave crimes destined to put us away for a long time if we were found guilty.

One day I was on my way to collect my dinner when an inmate who was standing at the top of the stairs outside my cell, polishing, said to me in a low voice, "Keep your chin up. We're seeing about all this." I said nothing back to him, just smiled. I was greatly comforted by his kindness. Maybe, just maybe there were people out there who didn't believe we committed this crime, who perhaps didn't swallow the press coverage quite so easily. I never saw this prisoner again, but I often wondered about him.

Some time later the *Irish Press* published a news item by Michael Farrell, "Warders Beat Remand Men." They described the information as coming from an eyewitness. We were all pleased; but the police brutality and savagery that forced us to sign confessions was worse than the beating we received from the Winson Green screws. Yet who was there to tell that tale apart from the six of us, and no-one was listening to our story.

The *Daily Express* ran an editorial about the merits of hanging. Eileen told me that after one visit she went home and switched on the television and they were debating hanging for IRA crimes. The anger expressed towards us inevitably affected our families. Sandra Hunter's house was ransacked; she had to leave the house, fleeing with her three young children. John Walker's wife and children returned to Derry, except for his eldest daughter, Bernadette, who was married in Birmingham. (Bernadette and her in-laws, the Hoctor family, were in the months and years to come a great source of support and help to Eileen, Sandra, and Kate, making her home available for them to meet each other and share their concerns and worries.) Billy's wife, Nora, and her children stayed initially with his family in Belfast. It was a very stressful time as innocent wives and children were forced to uproot themselves from their homes, schools, and jobs. Eileen and Geraldine had nowhere else to go: my family were in Belfast and Eileen's in Mayo, and neither could help much.

As it turned out, Eileen lost her job as a schools dinner lady. After I was arrested she went into work. All the talk was about the bombings; the women were very upset and angry. She went to the union, and they advised her that she should go on paid leave for a while. She came back the following week. By now they all knew that her husband had been picked up for the bombings. The supervisor said to her, "You shouldn't have come back." She was sent home and was forced, in the end, to leave. Going home that night on the bus, two of her workmates with whom she had been very friendly turned their backs on her. Eileen felt terrible. Everything had changed for her overnight. She used to love her little job and, ironically enough, did a little bit of work for the union, collecting her workmates' union subs. Now she was unemployed. She never worked again. Who would have her? Left alone with only Geraldine's income as a clerk, Eileen had to make application for social security payments. She found it a humiliating experience. Friends who were close to her deserted her, though not all. Her friend May, whom she knew since they shared the same digs in the 1950s, stood by her, but few others did. Geraldine carried on in her job; only her close colleagues knew who her father was.

It was a lonely struggle. There was little contact with neighbours, except the immediate ones, who were considerate.

But in the early weeks Eileen and Geraldine hardly slept a wink, expecting every night to be invaded and the house attacked. It was in some ways more dangerous for our wives and children outside than for us inside. The screws often said we were better off in prison: we were "protected." It wasn't the kind of protection I appreciated, but considering Eileen's situation it was probably true.

My brother Tom worked in Birmingham, and some of his workmates knew me. Tom used the surname O'Callaghan, and when my name was published without the "O" not everyone made the connection. Nevertheless the anger felt towards the Irish in the factories frightened him. He came to see me once in Winson Green. It was a trying visit. The factory was quite close to the prison, and he could have been seen. Tom was a quiet man who lived alone with his wife; they had no children. In our young days we had been very close, and I was always deeply fond of him. Tom couldn't handle the brutality of prisons and screws and locked doors, and I found the visit a great strain. I urged him to say nothing in his job and not to come again; I'd understand. I never saw Tom again. He died in 1987.

At no time while we were on remand did any prison officials take time to tell us about the rights of remand prisoners. We had no idea of our entitlements. Every day they would call around and say, "Any petitions? Any applications?" None of us had a clue what it meant. We would just say "No" or not respond. It had nothing to do with us.

After a while we were allowed to walk around the yard in pairs. The only other concession we had was that we were allowed to have exercise around the wing landing if it rained. But our meetings were few and our opportunity to chat in any detail limited. Paddy was a fighter, and was already writing to this one and that one about our arrest. He was very encouraging, and not daunted in the slightest by the might of authority. All of us made it clear in our own way to the prison officials that we were innocent. Any official, high or low, who crossed my path got the same speech. They just turned a deaf ear.

Our trial preparations were dragging on, with lengthy arguments about where the trial should take place. Our defence wanted it moved from Birmingham, arguing that it would be impossible to get a fair trial there given the anger already expressed and the newspaper coverage. We were referred to in all the media long before we came to trial as the "Birmingham pub bombers" or the "IRA bombers." What chance had we? Our defence were also looking for witnesses, and at Billy's suggestion, put an advertisement in the papers calling for witnesses to come forward, but their efforts weren't very impressive.

When we got the deposition papers laying out the charges and our so-called statements, we just couldn't believe it. I read and re-read my statement aghast. It was evident that throughout my interrogation I could give the police no information about who planted the bombs, so they simply decided to make it up. Their lies were repulsive and evil; but the most damning fact of all was that the statement contained my signature. I was trapped. The words that would be my undoing didn't amount to more than a hundred or so. While waiting for the train in the bar at the station I was alleged to have noticed that "Walker and Hunter had got some white plastic bags. I hadn't seen them before this. When we were about to leave the bar Hunter gave us all a plastic bag with a bomb in and told me to go to the Mulberry Bush with him. I put my bomb on the main road side of the Mulberry Bush ... I didn't want to kill anybody. I am sorry. I've never done anything like this before. I'm not even a member of the IRA."

The other confessions were just as bad, just as full of lies. Billy was alleged to have said it was he who planted the bombs in the Mulberry Bush, and Johnny was alleged to have said that Gerry planted the bombs in the Tavern with him. I don't know how Gerry was supposed to have been in two places at once. In fact forensic scientists were to show that the bombs were not in plastic bags but in cases or holdalls of some kind. It was just lies, lies, lies.

We had few opportunities to discuss the statements together. When we did we alternated between despair and amusement at some of the content of the statements. The language some of us were said to have used could never have been ours. Irish people simply didn't talk like that.

Meetings with our solicitors during the run-up to the trial were frustrating and not very frequent. It was clear that they had problems; but our main anxiety was that the confessions should not be admissible because they were beaten out of us. Only four of us had made confessions: Billy, Dick, John, and myself. They failed to obtain a confession from either Gerry or Paddy. Paddy was savagely beaten and marked, his feet burnt—everything they could inflict on him they did, but they failed to get him to confess.

Although we seldom met for any length of time to talk things through, the lads retained a lot of humour, and the brutality and hatred of the prison population didn't get the better of us. We were always confident that the truth would come out at the trial.

During our seven months' remand we gradually established some routine. I got a radio in my cell, which I listened to long into the night. I wrote regularly to Eileen and Patsy. I never said much about my personal feelings: I couldn't bear the intrusion of the censors who read our letters. I referred over and over again to my innocence. I looked forward immensely to receiving their letters. Patsy was always cheerful and full of home news. She tried to get me a subscription to the *Irish News* but it was too expensive; much later, taking an interest in our case following my letter to them, they sent it to me free from the office, and reading about home football and other events in Belfast helped me escape the harshness all around me.

They relaxed the rules on association and we were able to talk more and exchange news after family visits. Our wives were in contact with each other through the visits and were lending one another some moral support. I know that the rejection of a few more friends and the inability of either of our families to help a lot created severe stress for Eileen. On her visits to the prison the sarcasm of the screws and their foul language really upset her. Eileen was almost fifty—a shy, private and modest Irishwoman. The body searches she had to go through every time she came were humiliating. She retreated into her home and hardly spoke to a soul except a few close friends.

We always referred to my coming out "when this is all over." We were both convinced the forthcoming trial would right all our wrongs.

We finally got a date for the trial: 9 June 1975. We won a small victory when it was agreed that we would not get a fair trial in Birmingham and that it would take place instead at Lancaster Castle, a hundred miles or so from Birmingham.

Some days before the trial date we were moved to Lancaster

Castle. Our families weren't told. Eileen rang Winson Green to enquire if I had been moved, because she saw some reference to it on the news. She gave my name, and they asked her if she meant "the bomber." In the meantime I was on my way to trial, hoping to receive justice and some recompense for seven-and-a-half months of misery and unjust imprisonment.

7

The Trial

Almost eight months after we were arrested we were transported to Lancaster for the trial. We were handcuffed as well as locked inside the prison vans, and our journey was made deliberately unpleasant and uncomfortable. When we arrived we nursed sore and bleeding wrists. We were examined by the doctor and offered tranquillisers; I heard him say to the screws, "Those men look terrible. Make sure they are given milk with their food." It was the first time anyone in authority had shown the slightest concern for us.

Lancaster Castle was described by one newspaper as "the ideal setting for the bombers' trial." It was built on the best defensive position in the city, and its location was an aid to the massive "security" operation. We were again placed in separate cells with empty cells between, and isolated in a separate wing of the prison.

Many months and several thousand pounds went into preparing Lancaster Castle for our trial. The general atmosphere was more civilised and the attitude of the governor and assistant governor more humane. I relaxed a bit and began to believe that I was reasonably safe from assault here. The food was a hundred times better than what we were used to in Winson Green.

We remained optimistic, and we were looking forward to the trial. I still had faith in British justice, and this hope, together with the devotion and love of our families, motivated me to keep going and not to just sit down and give up.

Our wives had been assured by the assistant governor at Lancaster that there would be no repeat of our treatment in Winson Green. A detachment of specially selected screws was brought in from Strangeways Prison in Manchester. They guarded us with the same attention they would have given a pack of hounds; it was clear, however, that they had instructions to be on their best behaviour.

The trial lasted forty-five days. There were 132 charges, twenty-one of which were of murder. We were to be tried by Mr Justice Bridge, with Thomas Russell and Harry Skinner for the prosecution. John Field Evans acted for Billy, Paddy, and me, and Michael Underhill for Gerry, Dick, and Johnny.

We were told that Mr Field Evans had only agreed to take our case if he could represent at least three of us on his brief. He conducted himself very professionally with all of us, but he certainly didn't come over as a man convinced of our innocence. He questioned whether I might have been drunk, and been involved by the others. Might this have been the case, he asked? I was hopping mad; I told him I was innocent and was not about to tell lies now. I had grave doubts about him after this. He also told us he didn't think he could get the confessions thrown out. Billy, Paddy and I discussed the situation, adamant that we wanted the confessions challenged and that they should not be admissible evidence. They were forced out of us. We wanted Field Evans to push to have them thrown out, but Billy was of the view that Field Evans wasn't able to get the confessions disregarded. Billy initially wanted us to change our barrister. However, as with everything to do with our trial preparation, it was all too late. The solicitors impressed upon us that with just days to go to the trial we could not change barristers now. We wouldn't have a hope of getting another one. We had to accept Field Evans and hope he could do something in court, though we were not optimistic. Understandably, we were very frustrated.

The entire country, led by the media, believed we were guilty, and we were lucky to get anyone to represent us.

On the first morning of the trial we were up early. My nerves were in shreds. I ate nothing. I took the tranquillisers offered to me—anything would do to calm me down. Nevertheless, incredible as it may seem, I was looking forward to the trial. It was our first public opportunity to explain our side of the story.

A silence descended as we entered the court. My heart was thumping. The sight of all those people with their contemptuous glares fixed on us made me realise that we really were the most hated men in Britain. We were ushered to our seats, and, surprisingly, we were allowed to sit beside each other; that was comforting.

The usher commanded everyone to rise, and the judge made his grand entrance. He took his seat on a throne, high up over the court, from where he could look down on the assembled minions. His very appearance, dressed up in a gown and wig, with officials attending him even to the extent of helping him into his chair, added to the image of a god or a king. What would he know about our plight? Would he care?

The defence and prosecution lawyers sat alongside each other.

There seemed to be dozens of them, also dressed up in wigs and gowns. Sometimes they looked like members of two friendly football teams, with lots of smiles and comradely exchanges. Our lives were at stake, but for them it was just a job. The media people sat behind us; as the days went on, their numbers diminished. Directly across from us sat the jury, a dozen or so expressionless people.

A miserable six or seven seats were reserved for our families, and they were required to take turns sitting in the court. They were placed to the side of us, and we had to strain our necks to see a friendly face. Eileen and Geraldine were determined to avoid being photographed by the papers; when they decided not to attend the court I was relieved, even though it would have been comforting to have them there. It was more important for me that they protect themselves. Patsy came over during the last week of the trial, and she and Eileen came together to the court, always being careful to avoid the press photographers. We were allowed hurried visits every day after the court retired.

Three other men were on trial with us, charged with conspiracy to cause explosions, although they had no connection with us. We applied to have our case heard separately, but this was refused. We deeply resented their presence, but we could do nothing about it. I believe that having them there was a constant suggestion to the jury that somehow we were connected with them. I cannot honestly say I remember the details of what took place during those forty-five days. I was there in a physical sense, but it was hard to keep up with some of the procedures. I was often very tired, sometimes in a kind of trance. When the prosecution had the floor, the strain of listening to all the lies for hour upon hour was too much. There were times when the trial had some meaning, especially when we were in the witness box ourselves; but for most of the time we were silent participants in a drama in which we were the main characters.

After about four days of hearing statements from witnesses who were not going to appear in person, the Home Office forensic scientist, Dr Frank Skuse, was called. The court used scientific language I had never heard before and could never have understood. The judge declared his ignorance too (though it didn't stop him butting in). Skuse testified that he had found evidence of substances used in making explosives on Paddy and Billy. There was no scientific evidence against myself, Gerry, or Richard, while Johnny was found to have slight traces of nitrate ions on his hands, according to Skuse.

The defence called another forensic scientist, Dr Hugh Black, who, as far as I could understand it, maintained that there were other substances that would have given the same result. I thought Black was doing well, but the judge wasn't keen on him and started to interfere with the questioning process. Russell, aided by the judge, didn't allow Black the opportunity to elaborate. The whole business ended up with Black almost apologising to the judge for interrupting him! There was no possibility that any of us had been near explosives. I didn't need to understand the finer details.

Led by Billy Power to a great extent, we continued to push for the confessions to be thrown out. Finally Field Evans had a go. The judge decided to conduct a trial within a trial, and after eight days of deliberations he ruled that the confessions were admissible. He said that many of the allegations made by us against the police were of the most bizarre and grotesque character, and that if we were telling the truth he would have to accept that "a team of officers ... had conspired among themselves to use violence on the prisoners and to fabricate evidence." Of course that was in fact our case. He made lots of other comments as well, but the main outcome was defeat for us. We were finished.

The West Midlands police were called, and one after the other they came and told their story. If they got into difficulties they looked at their notes. They never went into detail, never elaborated, and that way they didn't trip themselves up. They rarely looked up at us or at anybody in the court: they either stared into their notebooks or looked blankly at the barrister asking the questions. They were obviously practised and experienced police officers, and the court atmosphere didn't intimidate them in the least.

Their most senior officer, George Reade, who led the investigation, gave his evidence. He told the court he had no knowledge of any assault, however mild. I never had him as an investigator, and therefore had no personal experience of him, though I heard about him from the other men.

We were each called to the witness box twice, by the defence and the prosecution. We received a slightly easier and more considerate time—as would be expected—from our defence barrister. We hardly knew the man—not the way you should get to know a person in whom you are trusting your life.

For all of us, the assaults and interrogation methods were what we most wanted to be questioned about. I spent a day and a half in the witness box. I did the best I could, but the questions centred mainly around my confession. It was so difficult to explain, even more so since the prosecution at least never allowed time for much elaboration. My efforts met with constant interruptions. I recollect Russell coming up close to the box, showing me the damned statement, and asking, "This is your signature, is it not?" "Yes, but—" "You didn't have violence inflicted on you, yet you signed." I tried to explain to this heartless man that with no sleep and no food, the threats and the mental terror, I would have signed anything in the end to escape. It was hopeless. He didn't want to hear the truth.

The prosecution frightened the life out of me by suggesting that I was responsible for planting a third bomb, which had failed to go off. After all, Russell suggested, none of the others could have done it, since they were on a train at the time. They also suggested that I had given the telephone warning. I heard my voice rise above a normal tone for the first time in months. I yelled at him, and cried out my innocence again. "I had nothing to do with planting that or any other bombs. I know nothing about making phone calls." I added for good measure that I had just spent seven months in prison for nothing. Bridge intervened, beside himself with indignation. How dare I or anyone behave like that in his court! He didn't care, he said, if I had spent seventeen months inside: he wouldn't accept that kind of behaviour.

My defence came to my rescue and, bowing to the court, apologised for what I said. Field Evans felt bound to explain that there was no reference to the third bomb in the charges against me. He didn't, of course, share my frustration or anger. Russell's accusations had seriously undermined me, but I just had to take it and carry on answering his questions, which after this little episode I found very difficult to do. I was conscious that the jury heard his allegations and would take note. Just my word against his!

While I was still in the witness box with Russell interrogating me, his colleague, Harry Skinner, sat directly behind him and fixed his eyes on me and never moved, staring me out. I was reminded of the police interrogation: they too used this method. The effect on my nerves was devastating. I tried to look away, but each time I looked up to respond to Russell, Skinner's eyes were fixed on me. I was amazed to find a senior man of the law resorting to such crude tactics. Skinner knew from my evidence and my very appearance that I was a man of a nervous disposition and that it was easy to undermine me. Here I was explaining how my confession was signed as a result of mental torture while I was being confronted with the same treatment in the court!

Dr Harwood, who examined us when we arrived at Winson Green, gave evidence that what he saw of our injuries proved to him at least that we had already been beaten up before we arrived. But Bridge wasn't having any of it, and he proceeded to diminish Dr Harwood in the eyes of the jury and to humiliate him. He even cast doubt on his medical competence.

Each of us, I suppose, coped with giving evidence in our own way. Billy was called before me, and being the first he had no idea what to expect, but he handled it well. In the months leading up to our trial both Paddy and Billy came to understand a lot of the scientific evidence; Paddy had spent his remand days writing to all and sundry and carefully reading the deposition papers. To an ordinary bloke like myself their knowledge and self-confidence were impressive. Dick was confident in the box as well. But by the time they had finished with us we were all mentally exhausted, and resigned to our fate.

We had the opportunity to talk to each other after the court every day. In the beginning we would go over and over what was said, analysing answers and commenting on this or that witness; but towards the end of the trial we gradually stopped talking about it. It was too painful. We all withdrew into ourselves, and the only bit of sunlight we experienced was the prospect of visits from our families. Every day Eileen would scan all the papers. Most of them were awful: hardly readable. Peter Chippindale in the *Guardian* was an exception: he gave accurate reports, and was sceptical. Despite this Eileen still felt that we would be found not guilty. We even arranged to meet at a particular place in Lancaster. No-one would know, and that way we would avoid the media.

The prison authorities were obsessed with security. We were guarded day and night; about twice a week we were required to move cells. The only reason they ever gave us was that one word, "security." It really got on our nerves, and contributed of course to our overall distress by the end of the trial.

I occasionally spent my time in the court observing the different characters in this drama. The judge frequently took over the cross-examining himself; he would make mincemeat of some witnesses, as he did to the prison doctor. Dr Harwood is dead now, and never lived to see his evidence proved to be true after all.

The jury changed in their demeanour during the trial. Their early indifference went; but they never appeared well disposed towards us. One juror fell asleep frequently. There were coughs and snorts from them when we were giving evidence; the few good points we were able to make would provoke pretended indifference, like staring up at the ceiling. By the end of the trial they appeared to me unashamedly biased against us. I had no doubt what their verdict was going to be.

The judge took three days to sum up. He lost his voice at one stage; but he could have saved his breath. He suggested to the jury that we were lying, that the police couldn't possibly conspire to lie and perjure themselves on the scale suggested by us. He slated the defence scientist, Dr Black, who he said had no experience and couldn't offer any satisfactory explanation to challenge the methods used by Dr Skuse; if Dr Black was right it meant that Dr Skuse had spent most of his professional life wasting his time. The contradictions in our confessions were put there deliberately, he suggested, when we realised the enormity of our crime. And on and on he went.

The jury took six hours to come to a unanimous verdict. The foreman of the jury was required to repeat the word "guilty" over and over again to each of the charges. I thought he would never sit down and shut up. "Guilty, guilty, guilty." The words were repeated over and over again. Why did they have to do it like this? I thought I would go mad.

The judge called out all our names and proceeded, "You stand convicted ... on the clearest and most overwhelming evidence I have ever heard, of the crime of murder. The sentence for that crime is not determined by me. It is determined by the law of England. Accordingly, in respect of each count each one of you is now sentenced to imprisonment for life.—Let them be taken down." I was numb and devastated, hardly able to stand up, but I said a quiet prayer of thanks that hanging no longer existed. The other fortunate—and under the circumstances surprising—thing was that the judge did not make a recommendation that life should mean "imprisonment for your natural life," though the significance of this was not uppermost in our minds as we left the dock to begin our sentence.

During the judge's address the police goaded us and openly mouthed abuse, no doubt hoping to provoke us into some gesture of defiance. None of us said a word.

Mr Field Evans saw myself, Paddy and Billy for about half an hour. He expressed his sympathy, but he was hardly what I would call moved by our plight. The man seemed hardly to know us, and, having used our surnames in court all the time, had a job remembering our first names at times. An appeal would be lodged immediately. We would get legal aid, of course; and that was about it. You could almost hear him saying, "Off you go now."

Eileen, Geraldine and Patsy were not in court to hear the verdict. They spent the day in Morecambe, walking round and drinking endless cups of tea in cafés. In the late afternoon they watched the news on a television in a shop window. They couldn't hear the sound properly, but enough to learn that we were found guilty on all counts and that we had got life imprisonment. Sitting later for nearly an hour on a bench in the centre of Morecambe, none of them knew what to do or where to go next. Eileen didn't know if we were still in Lancaster, but she guessed that we were probably moved.

The *Lancashire Evening Post* next day summed it all up. "Guilty: pub terror bombers get life. Evidence over-whelming, says judge."

8

TO PRISON FOR LIFE

Just a few hours after the verdict we were already on our way to begin a life in prison. We had no idea where we were being taken. Whisked away at top speed, we left behind us the screaming crowds who surrounded the prison. "Hang the bastards! Hang them, hang them!"

Richard and I travelled together; I wasn't sure if the others were following on in separate vans. We had a screw each for company, to whom we were handcuffed. Every now and then the entourage would stop and a new shift of escorts would take over. Helicopters followed overhead. It was a gigantic and expensive charade, but no doubt the great British public were impressed with this display of "security" as we sped across the English countryside.

It was a dreadful journey. Over and over again I said to myself, I'm going to prison for life—for a crime I had no part in and knew nothing about. Poor Eileen! What would happen to her and to Geraldine? We would never share a life together again. Geraldine would probably be married in a few years, and Eileen would be alone. Unlike the other men's families, my family all lived in Belfast and had hardly ever been out of it. They were still coping with the shock of my awful trial and conviction. Geraldine was the only offspring from all my brothers and sisters. She had no immediate relatives near her own age to talk to. There were no cousins, no brothers or sisters. Eileen's family lived in the west of Ireland, far removed from our troubles and unable to leave their homes and jobs for any length of time to come to Eileen's aid. There was nothing practical they could do. They lived too far away and had their own lives to live. Eileen was very much alone and would simply have to learn to cope somehow. I was deeply conscious of her difficulties as I contemplated her future without me.

I was older than the other five men, but still only forty-three. I had so much of my life yet to live. I thought of all the things that were never to be now. I would never live in my own home again; never enjoy the simple pleasures of life, like going to a football match or for a drink with friends or just a walk in the park with my daughter. I would never again be a free man.

The principal officer didn't waste his opportunity to rub our noses in it. "You'll be digging ditches now," he said. "I won't be digging no ditches!" Richard responded angrily. He always had great fight in him. Nobody put him down. It was good to observe the screws not getting the better of him, with words at least.

We arrived late at night at a prison in Bristol. As the van pulled up, all the memories of our arrival at Winson Green came flooding back; I prayed that we wouldn't have another "reception committee." I was surprised to see Paddy, still handcuffed to a screw, emerge from another van that pulled up a few minutes after ours. The more of us together the better I liked it.

Our particulars and other formalities were dealt with quickly.

We surrendered all our possessions: watches, cigarettes, and so on. We were also required to hand in every stitch of our clothes in exchange for prison issue. The prison clothes were clean but threadbare, and rough to the skin from years of wear and wash. They hadn't got my size of shoes, and I had to make do with the next size up; they felt like clogs. But it was the least of my concerns. So far we were there an hour and no assaults and little verbal abuse had taken place. I was surprised and relieved.

The prison was quiet; everyone was locked up. We were taken to our cells. The screw said very little: just gave me instructions about making up my bed and where the bucket was, and left. The door slammed behind him. I was "banged up" for the night, and here I was for the rest of my life.

My new surroundings were of little interest to me, but I was pleased to see that my cell had some space. It had a peep-hole in the door, and I could see three people in the cell opposite me. At least I had some privacy. I crashed onto the bed completely shattered, and fell asleep. Thus ended my first day as a convicted prisoner.

On our first morning we were called to the assistant governor's office and given a lecture about accepting what had happened and obeying the rules. We wouldn't be there long, he said, just until they found a suitable place in a top-security prison.

I was sent to visit a prison psychologist, a very nice young woman, but I didn't like what she asked of me. I was required to do some exercises with toy bricks. She went on to ask me questions, addressing me as she would a simpleton. I became sullen and mute, and she quickly gave up. I couldn't see the point of it. Was it possible, I wondered, that they regarded people who declared their innocence as in need of psychological treatment?

Our routine was to be different from that of all the other prisoners. We dined alone in our cells, spoke to no-one, and just the three of us exercised out in the yard, alone except for the screws who were always present. For our exercise we were required to walk round and round the yard, but at least we could talk to each other, and I was glad of Paddy and Richard's company.

Our first walk in the exercise yard was strange. There were lots of screws, and I had come to expect that, but no-one else was around; yet I felt as if the whole prison population was looking at us. As we walked into the yard I saw a noose hanging down over the door frame, and the screws just left it there, sniggering when they saw it. It was sick, but we ignored it.

A few mornings later, out on exercise, a screw started to whistle "The Sash My Father Wore." No doubt it was meant to insult us, but it didn't offend me in the slightest. It's a nice tune. Paddy, knowing I used to play the harmonica, said it was a pity I hadn't got it with me; I could have accompanied it nicely.

I went back to my cell on the second morning to find that someone had peed all over the floor. I was revolted by it, but said nothing to the screws—it could have been one of them. I just wiped it up and carried on.

We were not allowed to associate with the other prisoners, and that suited me fine. The few occasions I encountered them so far were not encouraging. Yes, we were better off alone. Some prisoners when accompanied by screws felt it was safe to be abusive and spiteful to us. I never responded, but I despised the prisoners who did this. To me they were worse than screws, because I thought they should show solidarity with other prisoners instead of licking and crawling round the screws to win their favour.

The chaplain paid me a visit when I had been there a week or so. He was a bit awkward. "I've just been to see your friends."

"Have you?" I asked.

"Yes." He coughed, looking very uncomfortable.

"Then you know the situation?"

"What do you mean?"

"You'll know we didn't do this."

His reaction was that of an upper-class Englishman. "Come, come, come."

I was livid. "Are you insinuating that we did this? It certainly sounds like it to me. If I can't get a man of the cloth to believe in me I've no wish to carry on this conversation. I want to be left alone." I showed him the door.

He was shocked by the directness of my words. So was I.

The next night a screw opened my door and said in an authoritative voice, "The priest wants to speak to you." I'm in trouble now, I thought, for being outspoken to the chaplain.

He stood looking very embarrassed, not able to look me in the eye. He made a feeble attempt to apologise. "Perhaps," he said, "I was a bit hasty last night."

Well, I wasn't going to relent. "You said what you thought, and that's that. As far as I'm concerned you believe I'm guilty. You're not the only one. I'm not lying to you. I'm innocent."

He made matters worse. "It's quite natural to be upset."

"Jesus!" I thought aloud. "Upset is hardly the word, when people like you don't believe me. You condemned me without showing any willingness to listen."

He left shortly afterwards. I knew that the outside world had been convinced by the media of our guilt. However, I expected the chaplain to be a bit more compassionate and more discerning. My faith in the mercy of God declined rapidly. I resolved after that visit that I would use every opportunity when I met people in authority to insist on my innocence, and just keep on saying it over and over again. The priest was my first shaky start.

At Paddy's suggestion we started writing letters to MPs, civil liberties people, and anyone in Ireland we thought might be receptive. Paddy was great at this; almost the moment we arrived in prison he was in action. On our first walk together he told us he was going to write to this one and that one. Paddy talked a lot, but I knew he was determined and he meant business. It kept us going in that first week. Richard wrote very well also; he drafted a very good letter to the Irish Government, which we all signed. Our letters didn't insist that the reader should believe we were innocent just on our say-so but that they look a bit closer at the facts of our case.

We were frequently disappointed. I wrote to the MP for my constituency, Julius Silverman. He wrote a curt letter back, offering no hope unless new evidence came to light. We had been "fairly tried," and there was little he could do. No apologies, no sympathy, and no response to my invitation to come and see me. That letter was a waste of time.

I wrote to the *Irish News*, my home newspaper. They published the letter, although it didn't yield an immediate response. However, I kept up my letters, and I began to like writing and got the hang of it. It was a great thrill when they finally published them.

There were new rules now that we were convicted, no longer on remand. Our wives had to have a "visiting order" to see us, and we had to make formal application each time. Unlike remand prisoners, who could be visited by simply calling to the prison, convicted prisoners were limited to so many visits a month or a year; if you ran out you had to wait till your entitlement to VOs was renewed again. I didn't have too many problems, as Eileen couldn't make many trips from Birmingham to Bristol.

It was difficult to get a lot of information from Eileen on her visits. They were what were described as "closed visits," in a separate room and always accompanied by one or two screws, and we were always closely observed. Private conversations, either through visits or letters, were impossible. She wouldn't have said anything in front of the screws about any work she was doing on our behalf, for fear it might rebound on me.

During our three months in Bristol I remember a discussion on the radio about hanging for certain types of crime; we would have been high on the list. Even though we were already sentenced, it crossed my mind that if they brought back the death penalty we might be hanged. You can become almost paranoid in prison, especially when you feel the whole world would regard such a death sentence as just. It haunted Eileen. Just after we were picked up the newspapers were full of demands for death for "IRA bombers," and prison staff and police who crossed our path since we were picked up in November 1974 often said to us, "You should be hanged." They were reflecting the wishes of ordinary people, and that's what was so awful.

And yet during this three months a few prisoners changed their attitude towards us, though most continued to be hostile. The first time was when we were being taken by screws to the canteen. An Irishman gave me an encouraging nod and half smiled. It meant a lot.

A Scottish prisoner stopped us once as we were being escorted to the library. "Did you know you're not getting your full ration of food?" It seems we should have been getting soup with our dinner, and the prisoners in the kitchen were short-changing us. It was sorted out; and from that point the prisoners' little revengeful acts against us gradually ceased. But we never learnt to trust them, and I lived in permanent fear of attack. We were asked once by the screws if we wanted to go and watch a film with the rest of the inmates. We would have liked to go, but Paddy advised against it. It could be a set-up. "You'll be okay," the screws assured us. "Nothing will happen." But we didn't go. We couldn't trust the screws or the inmates.

Paul Hill, one of the Guildford Four, came to Bristol while the three of us were there. He too had been wrongfully convicted, and we fully understood what he was going through. He was allowed to exercise with us. Paul was a young man, well able to speak up for himself, and for others. The inmates all wanted to see what a "natural lifer" looked like (the judge had recommended that he should remain in prison for the rest of his life). I think Paul spoke his mind to the governor and the screws about our innocence. He didn't talk much about himself or his case, but he conceded not an inch to the screws, and he got a very hard time as a result. He had determination and guts.

Our wing was used for what were called "lie-downs," prisoners being isolated as punishment, or at their request for their own protection. In the short time we were there I became friendly with a few inmates on "lie-down." They would shout out from their cells and indicate that they were being friendly, asking for fags and so on. Every friendly gesture, however small and whatever the circumstance, was welcome, and I suppose its importance magnified beyond reality.

Bristol was an old and shabby place. The facilities were poor.

The food was adequate, but not plentiful. We weren't working, which meant we were not entitled to any wages. We got a pittance called "wing money," about 80p a week—not enough to keep you in "skins" (cigarette paper) if you were a smoker. Richard was always gasping for a cigarette. He used to have to resort to toilet paper when he ran out of skins. He frequently went without tobacco, and he would be very troubled for the want of a cigarette in the evenings.

There was little for us to do in Bristol. We spent almost twenty-three hours a day in the cells. I listened to the radio morning, noon, and night. I wasn't a great reader; I suppose if I read a bit more it would have helped pass the time. I would read the *Daily Express*, because it had the best sports news; but mostly I was bored, and frequently depressed. I hated Bristol. I couldn't wait to leave it.

On 6 November 1975, just three months after my arrival in Bristol, I got a tap on the shoulder from a screw. "Get your gear together. You're on the move." Within half an hour Paddy and I were on our way to a new prison, we didn't know where. I heard someone say "the Island." We were taken to the ferry going across to the Isle of Wight, and I learnt what this meant. Bristol was behind me, and was I glad to see the back of it!

There are two prisons on the Isle of Wight; we were placed one in each. After stopping off at Parkhurst Prison to deposit Paddy, they carried on to Albany Prison with me. We were finally separated.

9

ALBANY PRISON, 1975–1982

I don't know what I expected to see—another grey old prison, I suppose, like Winson Green and Bristol. Instead I saw a modern building, extending in a semicircle for miles, just off the main road. At the reception desk the screws addressed me in a normal tone of voice. There were no raised voices, no commands. I was politely requested to hand over my possessions. They were businesslike and not openly hostile; but despite the politeness all around, I remained suspicious.

I had a cell to myself. It was modern and clean, though smaller than my cell in Bristol. It had the basics, a bed and a table, and bare walls, clean and surprisingly free of graffiti. The window was high up and looked out on the main road; I could see people standing at the local bus stop. I stood and looked round me, and I said to myself: Cooped up here for life—never. I'd go mad.

Albany is a top-security prison. All the internal doors are electronically controlled, closing behind you with a click—a new experience for me; I had got used to the jangling of keys as doors were crashed open or shut by screws. I knew this new system would take some getting used to. At six o'clock that evening, about an hour after I arrived, a green light went on in the cell, and the lock clicked open. This was "association time," or recreation time in other words. I had no desire to associate, and I wasn't all that keen on recreation either. It suddenly dawned on me that I was no longer segregated from the other prisoners. What's more, I was on my own. All the fears about being beaten up came flooding back.

At least segregation had served some useful purpose. Everywhere we went in the prison world for the past twelve months the hatred of the prison population was evident. Given the opportunity, screws and inmates abused us. Convinced that the same would happen here, I stayed in my cell, though I knew I couldn't do this for ever.

Some time later an inmate came into my room. He encouraged me to come out with him, and he indicated that the republican prisoners knew of my arrival. I would, he assured me, be okay. When I appeared, there were a lot of curious stares in my direction; I heard remarks about being one of the "Birmingham gang." I looked ahead of me and said little, but I acknowledged the curious and half-friendly nods in my direction.

At the close of association time I was eager to return to my cell and to relative safety, relieved to have escaped being beaten up. But I needn't have been so anxious. They treated me well, and there was no aggression shown towards me. I was grateful too for the republican prisoners' concern. It certainly smoothed my path. But I didn't talk to them that evening. I couldn't; I had nothing to say.

A few days later Seán Campbell, a republican prisoner, came over and shook hands with me. "We know you're not one of us and we know you're innocent. As a matter of fact you don't even have to talk to us if you don't want to." "My politics," I said, "are completely different from yours, but it wouldn't stop me saying hello to you." It might have been easier for me if I had been able to link up, as it were, with the republican prisoners. After all, they were Irish, like myself; but it would only have compounded my problems. The authorities viewed me as a republican activist; I wasn't, and never had been, and it was important to establish that from the start, however isolated it left me—though despite my decision, the screws' ability to comprehend the subtlety of my actions was nil.

Later the republican prisoners let it be known to me that I would be better off getting transferred from A wing to E wing, where I would be "safer." Someone was going to have a word with the governor about it.

I walked round alone on my first exercise. I kept looking over my shoulder. I heard the screws talking about me, and saw them pointing their fingers in my direction. Inmates just stood and watched me. I felt uncomfortable, but I wanted the walk, and the fresh air felt very good on my face. An Irish lad came over to me; he just said hello, but his voice was reassuring. He didn't dare walk round with me, for fear of association with a notorious bomber!

If you have to spend time in prison, Albany was certainly a fairly reasonable place to be. The sea air was much fresher and more bracing. It was physically more comfortable, and it was less regimented than other prisons. They didn't make a big deal out of carrying out domestic chores: making the bed, tidying the cell, and so on. And, unlike old prisons such as Bristol and Winson Green, there was night sanitation at 10 p.m., with proper toilet facilities. During association time we could choose to go out on exercise or stay in the games room, watch television, use the gym, or just do nothing. Some guys never went outside the door; they were the colour of white paint.

The first six months were the hardest. I tried to keep active, and looked forward to my daily walk round the grounds. But they were lonely walks. For the first two years of my imprisonment in Albany I walked alone. I would walk round and round for half an hour and not speak to a soul. Screws were constantly observing me and who I might talk to; prisoners due to be considered for parole were understandably anxious not to blot their copybooks.

I was desperately depressed and unhappy in those first six months. I dreaded waking up in the morning. The reality of being a "lifer," locked up in an institution for ever, was hard to contemplate at any time, but in the early light of day it was hardest of all. There were mornings when I would have preferred not to wake up.

There were many people in Albany who were mentally unstable. At night I could hear them screaming and talking to themselves, or sometimes laughing hysterically. It was a strange, terrible sound, bouncing off the walls and echoing all over the prison.

Our appeal was due in March 1976. It was grounded mainly on how Mr Justice Bridge had conducted himself in his summing up. Our defence argued that Bridge was biased, that he unduly influenced and misdirected the jury. He had failed to accept the possibility of accidental explosives traces; and we argued that he was hostile to certain parts of our defence evidence.

Losing the appeal came as no shock. No-one expected us to win; but all the same it was a low point for me. The appeal judges threw out all our arguments; the only concession was that Bridge "unhappily went too far" in his treatment of Dr Harwood. Lord Chief Justice Widgery dismissed our beatings as a "knocking about" that didn't go "beyond the ordinary." He didn't think the scientific evidence was greatly important—contradicting Bridge, who described the scientific evidence as "absolutely critical." Bridge, the appeal judge said, didn't overstep the mark with the jury; on the contrary he had told them they were free to make up their own minds. Our appeal was emphatically dismissed.

I yearned for my home and to be returned to my family. To go back to normality would be all I would ever have asked for again. I doubted my ability to survive the mental torture I experienced every day; but the reality was that people did survive. The republican prisoners were an example. The system didn't seem to defeat them or bring them down, even though it was no secret that the screws hated them. If I was told then that I would live to endure many more years of imprisonment I would not have believed it.

I received medication that helped to control the depression and anxiety, though it did little to subdue the pain, which continued in different degrees throughout the day and night. I was often glad to have an extra tablet the medical people didn't know about. I also had a brief spell of psychiatric treatment. I had little faith in psychiatrists of any kind. As far as I was concerned there was nothing wrong with me psychologically, I was simply innocent; if they had opened the gates and released me I would have been as right as rain.

I had a persistent longing to talk about my innocence to anyone who cared to listen. They, sadly, had no desire to share my concerns. I would make a simple statement, "I am an innocent man," and they would pull a face or make a remark, "Not all that again, Callaghan!" It was a taboo subject. The senior prison staff were prepared to talk to me for as long as necessary about any topic I cared to raise, except the one uppermost in my mind: my innocence and wrongful imprisonment. If I persisted, which I frequently did, they would become mute and unresponsive. It was important for me that the authorities anywhere I was to be sent should know that I wasn't accepting for one minute my conviction. The prison staff, from the governor down, advised me that it would be easier if I accepted my fate and got on with it, but I couldn't.

I used my letters to speak about our innocence, and precious little else. I never let up. It became an obsession to write about it over and over again. I repeated myself so many times in my letters to Eileen and Patsy and anyone else I corresponded with that the censors must have been browned off reading them. I wrote a lengthy letter to Jean Beggs (Murphy), which I suppose was meant to address through her my own people in Ardoyne. The papers were so awful, vile and full of hateful accusations, even before we went to trial, that I needed to know for my own peace of mind what people thought, especially people like Jean and her family. I was rewarded a few days later when I received a lovely warm letter in return. She always knew I was innocent and never believed I or the others had anything to do with planting explosives in pubs. She told me about her husband and her family, and gave me lots of news of interest to me. It made my day to receive that letter, and I read it over several times. Jean began to write regularly, as did her daughters when they got older. I looked forward immensely to those letters.

All letters were censored. Prisoners were restricted in what they could write. Any references to the conditions in prison or how the prison regime is run were prohibited. For prisoners with a grievance it was impossible to convey your concerns in letters that passed through the censors. Such restrictions and the knowledge that others were reading your private letters denied prisoners a basic human right to express their true feelings about anything of importance to them.

The Catholic chaplain changed while I was in Albany. The first chaplain was too old to care. He had been a prison chaplain for years and was past hearing the prisoners' pleas. He visited me a few times and we had polite, meaningless conversations. His replacement was an upper-class Englishman who would have a conversation one night and a few hours later forget your name. He would approach you on the landing and ask, "Who are you?" He wasn't stupid or even forgetful, just indifferent. He never bothered to get to know us or show any real interest in the spiritual well-being of the inmates. You would see him hobnobbing with the senior prison staff most of the time he was on the wing. He was just one of them.

I rarely attended Sunday Mass. It had lost all meaning for me. I didn't experience Christ's compassion in any Catholic chaplains I had met so far.

Prisoners were all categorised. I remember once in Winson Green asking Paddy what the term "Cat A" meant after I saw the words written up on doors in bold ink. "It's supposed to mean we are a danger to society. And you know what a lot of ballocks that is." I laughed at this directness. It was a preposterous thought to us all the same. I was a category A prisoner, "whose escape would be highly dangerous to the public or the police or to the security of the state, no matter how unlikely that escape might be." From what I experienced, the categories were designed to give certain prisoners additional annoyance as they served out their sentences, and especially so for category A prisoners. I was "on the book," which meant that throughout the day I was checked as I moved from one part of the prison to another or from one activity to another. I was escorted everywhere, and a book was signed at each stage. I had to change cells regularly, and they were frequently checked and my possessions searched. On visits I would be accompanied from the wing to the visiting areas by a screw and his dog.

Category A prisoners had only closed visits, which meant we had to suffer two or three screws accompanying us on every visit, which was held in a separate room. Everything we said or did was observed. The people who could visit me had to be approved and photographed by the police, and everyone who wasn't immediate family had to be vetted.

I was called out once from the exercise field by the security screws, who marched me back to my cell to explain tiny marks underneath my cell window. It was pathetic. I told them the marks were there when I came to the cell and that I wasn't interested in escaping over the wall: I would come out of prison the way I was put into it, through the courts, and with my name cleared.

In January 1976, just six months after our conviction, the Director of Public Prosecutions announced that fourteen warders from Winson Green were to go on trial, charged with assault. The police who interrogated us before our arrival at Winson Green were equally culpable, or indeed more so, because of the way they perjured themselves on such a grand scale at our trial: their lies sent us away for life. Nevertheless I was looking forward to the "screws' trial," as we called it. I didn't expect justice, but I was a different person from the one who appeared in court the last time. I was angry, and determined to be a lot more assertive about our innocence. I couldn't wait to be called to give evidence. I was no longer afraid or in awe of courts. The law wasn't on the side of the innocent working man—but then, was it ever? I had no doubt the warders would get off. No court would put them behind bars; but the outcome was immaterial compared with the opportunity it was going to give me to say what was on my mind.

The morning I was being taken to the screws' trial, I walked into the reception area and there was Paddy Hill sitting waiting for me, smoking a roll-up. He gave me a grin and a hug. He had lost a lot of weight, but he was as friendly and chatty as ever. Paddy entertained us all, including the screws, all the way up to Birmingham with his news and views on our case and life in Parkhurst. He never felt the restraint of screws listening to his conversation; he just carried on regardless.

I was placed in Long Lartin for the duration of the trial, but Paddy was only brought there for tea and was taken on to Leicester, much to his disappointment. Long Lartin was a modern prison, run more liberally than Albany, but I wasn't there long enough to get a taste for it. I didn't engage much with the other prisoners. Dick McIlkenny was there, but he was on a different wing. The few times I saw him he was always engaged in some activity or other. Dick busied himself in prison, always doing something with purpose. He seemed to have lots of company, and was well liked. He was an active prisoner—kept his mind busy. He had lost a lot of weight and looked a bit older since I last saw him in Bristol, but his personality, his strength of character and confidence in himself were still there.

The screws' trial lasted two weeks. My new solicitor, Brian Rose Smith, acted on my behalf and some of the others. He was good, and knew his stuff. I spent one day in court, but for me it was a landmark and gave me a self-confidence I hadn't got when I had given evidence in Lancaster. I had lived among all kinds of men in a violent world where the only way to survive was to toughen up and be strong. I had learnt to be more confident, and no longer feared authority.

I was bursting to speak; I hardly gave the prosecution a chance to begin their questions when I launched in. "I want to say something. I must say something. The police beat us up to get us to sign those so-called confessions, which they had made up. We're six innocent men, wrongly convicted." I gave further evidence that I knew in advance we were going to be beaten in Winson Green, and added that this was done to cover up the marks already on us from the police beatings. Asked what I thought of the bombings, I replied that I thought it was a terrible thing, but "we had nothing to do with it."

I felt jubilant after I stood down. It did me the world of good. I had planned for months that I would make a public statement about our innocence; it went better then I ever expected. Geraldine told me afterwards that the police and the press looked amazed. The press described it as an "outburst by Birmingham bomber," and others wrote, "Bomber accuses police of beating him." It was nevertheless reasonably well reported, and I know it raised a few questions.

I wasn't allowed to hear anything else of the trial. As soon as my evidence was completed I was taken back to Long Lartin, and later to Albany to continue my sentence. But I followed the trial in the papers, and it finally came to the question of who beat us first, the police or the warders. The prison officers' defence had called Dr David Paul, a consultant in clinical forensic medicine, who was asked to study pictures taken of us while we were in police custody, before we went to Winson Green. He concluded that there was evidence of marks to the face and eyes on all of us, some of which we ourselves had not even declared. He told the court that in his view the pictures showed injuries sustained before we went to Winson Green, though he agreed that to the untrained eye they would not necessarily have been spotted a few days after they were inflicted.

In the summing up of the five-week trial the judge drew the jury's attention to the screws' long and outstanding service and to the "class of men" making the accusations against them. It took a few hours for the jury to return a verdict of not guilty on all fourteen. I expected nothing else. But the judge agreed that someone beat us up, and the *Guardian* editorial asked the question the day after the verdict: "Who beat the bombers?" The *Irish Press* wrote: "The fact has to be faced that there are people in the prison service, a part of the law enforcement agencies, who are getting off scot free when they break the law. It is a matter which must cause uneasiness no matter where it happens."

Our lawyers advised us to sue the West Midlands and Lancashire police and the Home Office for assault. After the failure of the screws' trial to convict anybody of assault—despite the admission by the judge that somebody must have assaulted us—we had nothing left to argue in the courts. Suing the police was a long shot, and it was possible that we would not be allowed to proceed to a trial.

In a physical sense at least, I was beginning to settle in Albany. I still hadn't come to terms with being innocent in prison, but by keeping fit and active and staying out in the open when I could I was coping reasonably well. Prisoners began to associate with me more and more; it was no longer regarded as a risk to take a stroll round the exercise grounds with me. I began to take part in prison activities.

My walk in the open air became as essential to me as eating or sleeping. I remember on Christmas morning rushing towards the exercise door. I was late, and I heard a screw saying to another, "Doesn't look as if Callaghan is coming out this morning." There wasn't another soul looking for the exercise yard. I got there just in time. "Here I am!" I called out. I knew they could decide not to let me out if they wished. Despite the snow and wind I got a good three-quarters of an hour before they called me in. My coat was covered in snow and my face and hands were cold. I didn't care: I got my walk, Christmas or no Christmas. I heard an inmate call out from his cell window, "There he goes. The loneliness of the long-distance walker!"

Albany had good sports facilities, including a well-equipped gym and a purpose-built football ground. I played football every weekend. There was an inter-wing league, and there were even national matches between the English and Irish prisoners. Some of the republican prisoners were great footballers, very skilled, young, and fit. They were co-operative up to a point, but they really annoyed the prison authorities when they refused to represent the prison in an inter-prison league.

The screws never gave an inch and enforced the regulations to the letter when it came to the republican prisoners, which, as far as they were concerned, included me. Out on exercise the republican prisoners would keep their own company; they often stood in a circle in the centre of the exercise field just in conversation. I never joined them, though there was no animosity between us. It gradually became obvious that I was not one of them, and it came as no surprise to anyone inside or outside the prison when the IRA finally confirmed that none of us were ever members of the IRA.

I was eventually transferred to E wing, and life became more tolerable. There were a lot of Londoners in the wing; they were "in control." I found them easy to get along with, though they had an intolerance of particular kinds of prisoners—rapists, child murderers, and the murderers of old people—whom they wouldn't have on their wing. Every effort to mix inmates convicted of "nonce" (sex) crimes was thwarted. News of the arrival of a sex case on E wing was inevitably followed by some form of sabotage, usually a cell fire. Such prisoners were isolated and ill treated; it was a miserable existence for them on E wing, and a transfer was the inevitable outcome. After my own experiences, who was I to condemn any of these people? Who is to say for certain that they were guilty?

I found that the Londoners accepted me without too much hostility, though I was always on my guard. During the late 1970s there were several bombing episodes in England and in the north of Ireland. Prisoners reacted in the same way as the rest of the British population, and Irish prisoners, political and non-political, had to be on the look-out for fear of retaliation.

The prison authorities kept a tight grip on any kind of protest, and broke it up instantly. On the other hand, they wouldn't give a toss what happened among prisoners. I saw some terrible violence, one prisoner against another, and the screws behaved as if they had seen or heard nothing. Prisoners were capable of very spiteful acts of revenge; I have seen the occasional leg broken in a football game, and not because the perpetrator was in innocent pursuit of the ball. The screws were especially indifferent to the woes of Irish prisoners, be they political or not. But the inmates knew that the screws already gave us plenty of aggro.

The republican prisoners protested once over one of their group being put "on the block" (isolated), and they took over the wing. The authorities reacted with terrible violence. The "mufti squad," which included scores of screws from Albany and nearby Parkhurst Prison, steamed in and broke the group up. They beat the hell out of them, using their boots and fists. It created a terrible atmosphere in the prison afterwards.

The following night there was a small protest by some of the ordinary prisoners, strongly objecting to the violent way the mufti squad treated the republican prisoners. The screws expected me to join in; they even came to my cell door and asked if I would be joining it. I simply said no and closed the door. They couldn't understand my situation. I would never get involved in prison riots or protests: I had too much of a battle just proving my innocence. But I shared the anger of the other Irish prisoners. What the mufti squad did was utterly disgraceful; they had the authority to beat up people they despised.

Around this time I was out in the exercise yard and a screw from Belfast came up close to me. He was handling a dog, and encouraging the dog to go for me. "Who did you kill? How many did you murder, you IRA bastard?" I replied, "I haven't killed anyone. I'm an innocent man." He withdrew. I was surprised he went for me, because up to that time he never gave me the slightest hint that he even noticed me; I learnt later that he lost a relative in a recent explosion in Belfast. I reported the assault to the governor—not that I expected him to do anything. He didn't. Prisoners never get apologies, ever. The prisoners on E wing learnt of this assault and I was surprised at their concern. They were genuinely angry, and let the other screws know.

and Patsy could not communicate much
in either home.

y's efforts on my behalf, and I knew
that she cried every day over "our
as great: never complaining, and trying
ny sake. She was always full of gossip
k to talk about home, never daring to
a for fear the authorities would object.
e days about rights and privileges of
.

allenge the reasons for closed visits. I
governor, and I argued my case. "I'm
e through the courts. I'm not interested
mping walls. But I'm damned if my
the way from Birmingham to see me
hands or have a personal conversation.
is being punished along with me for
nmitted." He listened with impassive
a lecture about visiting rules and
prisoners, but he would see what he

open visit. I sensed I was winning.
me more confidence. The open visit
were more people in the room, more
children for the first time in nearly
as stimulating to see different faces,
niforms. Eileen and I could talk a bit
om drowned out our conversation a
awful lot, but gradually, over a few
e had been put in touch with a man
ppeared out of the blue to help us.

There were some interesting characters on E wing. Lifers
were easier to get along with. Two Londoners in particular, Billy
Gear and Tony Edlin, were the funniest men in the prison.
They mocked everyone, especially the screws and the toffee-
nosed senior officers. I got to work with them sometimes, and
they had me laughing so much that I could forget my troubles.
I made friends with a guy called Fletch. He was a seasoned
inmate; he only knew how to live a prison life. He knew how
to bend the rules, and showed me a few good tricks to ensure
my survival in prison.

I learnt from watching guys like Fletch and Billy Gear how
to "invest" the meagre money I earned working in various
jobs—"canteen money," as it was called. I wasn't a smoker, and
my food requirements were minimal. Others on the wing needed
my canteen money to buy cigarettes and other goods, and I was
able to do a little bit of dealing. I always liked a little gamble,
and it helped to pass the time.

I was willing to work. I worked first in the carpenters' shop;
I wasn't much of a carpenter, but it helped to be occupied,
learning something new. I was invited by a Scottish prisoner,
Ian Spence, to team up with him. "Stick with me and you'll be
okay," he promised. He was true to his word. In my early days
he showed me the ropes, came everywhere with me, and helped
pass the day telling yarns about the other inmates and the staff.
He was serving a long sentence and he knew everybody in the
prison world. He liked Irish people, and being a Scottish
Orangeman he knew a lot about the Orange lodges in Belfast.
He was a follower of pipe bands, and we had many long chats
about the different bands and competitions.

Friendships in prison were not easy. There was always an
element of mistrust, together with the need not to become too

involved in other people's lives; but Ian was a good sort. Though he wasn't that fond of exercise, he would walk round just the odd time. Later on, however, he took up running and became very good.

Later I befriended a man from Newry, and as time went by he and I would walk together. His family lived in London. We would talk about football, and about Ireland. Walking round the grounds on a summer evening you could forget for an hour at least that you were in prison. We seldom spoke about politics. He left abruptly, and I never heard from him again. He was a good man, who helped me a lot in my early years in Albany.

Sometimes an inmate got very short notice before his departure or transfer to another prison. He might have served ten or twenty years in Albany, then get half an hour's notice that he was being moved—"shanghaied," it was called. Inmates and pals were left to handle their loss alone in the privacy of their cells. There was little comfort from the prison staff or other inmates.

I was transferred to the "garden party," which was the first time a category A prisoner was allowed to work on an outdoor job. I was delighted: it suited my temperament entirely, and with the sea air, sunshine and no alcohol I was beginning to look healthy, though my mental turmoil was the same as ever. However, they weren't going to let me go, and I had to do whatever I could to survive. Co-operating with the system became essential, and it helped. I spent several hours a day out in the open, working in the prison grounds. I even got to do a course in horticulture, though I wasn't that interested in reading about gardening. I was just happy to do a bit and stay out in the open. Doing physical work helped keep my mind off things for a few hours every day.

Rose Callaghan (Hugh's mother) in the 1920s

Patrick Callaghan (Hugh's father),
British Army veteran of two world wars

Hugh, aged 14, in Belfast

Butler Street, Ardoyne and Holy Cross Church

Tom and Hugh Callaghan, St Chad's Dance Hall in Birmingham, about 1952

The young workman in Birmingham,
aged about 21

Eileen Callaghan, Hugh's wife, in 1955

In the back garden of the Callaghan home at Erdington, 1973—the scene of Hugh's arrest a year later

Hugh and Jackie at Wembley, March 1991

Hugh and daughter Geraldine (aged 4)

Football ground overlooked by Winson Green Prison—Hugh in local team with Belfast lads

At Kempton Park, 1 April 1991

Sean Healy and Hugh–saying thanks to a
campaigner *(Photo: Malcolm and Mel McNally)*

Billy Power with campaigner John Woodruff
and Hugh in Newark, Notts, 1991
(Photo: Malcolm and Mel McNally)

With the London campaign group, March 1991
(Photo: Terry Smith, The Irish Post)

Outside the Old Bailey,
March 1991
(Photo: London Independent)

Free!

At the Mansion House,
Dublin, May 1991, as
guests of the Lord Mayor

With President Robinson
at Áras an Uachtaráin,
May 1991

The six with Chris Mullin and Paul May *(Photo: Malcolm and Mel McNally)*

Bishop Edward Daly, Paul Murray
(Irish Embassy), Mgr. V Hannon, (Irish
Commission for Prisoners Overseas)
(Photo: Malcolm and Mel McNally)

At ease, 1991

With Fr Denis Faul at the London/Tyrone reunion,
May 1992
(Photo: Terry Smith, The Irish Post)

The Birmingham Seven! *(Photo: London Independent)*

Hugh with Sinéad Cusack, Kenneth
Griffith and Kenneth's daughter at
the Irish Book Fair, Camden Town,
March 1992
(Photo: Terry Smith, The Irish Post)

Billy Power's hand with
that bar of soap!

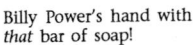

Enjoying life, May 1991 *(Photo:* Irish Post*)*

Outside Lancaster Prison, July 1992

A year after release (14 March 1992) *(Photo: London Independent)*

Mike Walsh was an extraordinary person who turned out to be a powerful source of help during my time in Albany. He was a member of the Labour Party in Birmingham and an active trade unionist. He was contacted by Eileen (he came from Mayo), and over several months he helped her find us a new solicitor. Mike Walsh arranged several meetings in various houses. None of the wives involved at that time doubted the risk he was taking. Neither his own wife nor people at his work-place had any idea he was helping Eileen or anyone accused of the Birmingham bombings. Being found out could mean losing his job and being ostracised. It was inconceivable to most ordinary Birmingham folk that anybody would want to help us in any way.

The meetings gradually included Sandra Hunter and Kate McIlkenny and her older daughters. The Hoctor family, whose eldest son was married to Bernadette Walker, John's eldest daughter, made their house available for meetings. Kate was living in terrible conditions at the time, in a squat, but she also provided a room. The meetings were get-togethers at first, providing the families with support and comfort. Gradually achieving mutual trust, Mike Walsh helped them with paperwork and letter writing, and also helped to establish how to go about taking a civil action, which we wanted to do against the police. He went to extraordinary lengths to help, travelling all over the place to find different solicitors who would agree to make legal aid applications. He spent days reading up on the law so as to be one step ahead of the others, who came to depend on him for advice. It was Mike Walsh who obtained the excellent solicitor Brian Rose Smith.

Eileen used to say about anything she needed to know, "I'll ask Mike Walsh." He was a man with courage, though he says himself that it was difficult at times. He also admitted being of like mind with the vast majority of people in Birmingham when we were convicted. When he got the call for help from Eileen he admitted to being very reluctant. He agreed to help, but expected it to be limited to helping Eileen change solicitors and helping the wives set up their own meetings in support of each other; then he would withdraw. That was a year ago. He told Eileen he could not walk away.

Two Irish priests, Father Denis Faul and Father Raymond Murray, published a book about our case. It was the first time our side of the story was revealed in print. I placed an order for the book in the library, but the prison authorities didn't want me to have it, and prevaricated for months. I eventually got the book, *The Birmingham Framework*, and read it in the privacy of my cell. On the front it said, "Six innocent men framed for the Birmingham bombings." I was delighted. These were brave men, who undoubtedly put their own reputations at risk to tell the truth about six innocent people the rest of the world believed to be mass murderers. This pamphlet was a landmark in the history of our fight back. The detailed study carried out by the priests on the confessions and the scientific evidence as they existed in 1975 was to prove an invaluable source of material for journalists, lawyers and writers who subsequently investigated our claims of innocence, including Chris Mullin. The priests' contribution to the understanding of our cause could never in my mind be overstated.

A few months after I read the book I received a beautiful letter, containing some money, from a Sister Sarah Clarke. Her letter was full of encouragement and belief in our cause; I was touched, and I read the letter several times. I started also to receive some mail from people in Belfast, all expressing their doubts about our trial and conviction. These letters from ordinary people were like a light shinning at the end of a long and very dark tunnel. Some of them were from people I knew, like Mary Mallon, whose father I used to do a paper round for as a lad in Ardoyne—a long time ago, yet she hadn't forgotten me.

I had a little radio that picked up RTE and Radio Ulster, though poorly. Later on a Belfast lad sold me a big radio for five pounds, which was a lot of money by prison standards, but that radio was worth its weight in gold to me. I could pick up the Irish stations perfectly. One programme I looked forward to in particular was "Sunday Club," which went out on Radio Ulster every Sunday night from eleven to twelve. It had a number of presenters, but when John Bennett took over it became a real pleasure. His style was so homely, and at that time of night he would play soft music and old tunes that I remembered from my youth. He used to read out requests, and if I recognised the place it would take me back to Belfast, thinking about the area and the people I once knew. I really felt at times far away from the reality of my prison cell, and for that hour I was back in Belfast. I kept special letters from friends or good people at home and read them during that hour. It was a whole sentimental journey, a form of escape I looked forward to every week.

One night I heard John Bennett say that this would be his last programme: that Radio Ulster were cutting the programme to save money. I was devastated. I never even bothered to switch on during the following weeks; then one night by chance I switched on to hear John Bennett's voice saying that they had had so many thousands of requests that money was found, and he was glad to be back among his friends. Was I pleased! I couldn't believe it. I rarely missed it after that. The programme still runs today, and John is still at the turntable.

In November 1977 our solicitors started a civil action against the West Midlands police for injuries received while we were in custody, basing our allegations on our own evidence and that of Dr David Paul. The Home Office admitted liability, but the police took steps to have the action struck off. The press howled about the "IRA bombers" being given legal aid. "Bombers to sue police—taxpayers to foot the bill. A quarter of a million to finance bombers' legal action."

Meanwhile the police's efforts to frustrate our attempts to sue them carried on. First our solicitors got the all-clear from one judge, Mr Justice Cantley. The police successfully appealed, and we lost our right to sue. The process took two years to reach this conclusion.

Lord Denning delivered the judgement. "If the six men fail, it will mean that much time and money have been expended by many people for no good purpose. If the six men win, it will mean that the police were guilty of perjury, that they were guilty of violence and threats, that the confessions were involuntary and were improperly admitted in evidence and that the convictions were erroneous. That would mean that the Home Secretary would either have to recommend they be pardoned or he would have to remit the case to the Court of Appeal. This is such an appalling vista that every sensible person in the land would say: It cannot be right that these actions should go any further." Adding self-congratulation to injustice, Denning continued: "This case shows what a civilised country we are. Here are six men who have been proved guilty of the most wicked murder of twenty-one innocent people. They have no money. Yet the state has lavished large sums on their defence ... In their evidence they were guilty of gross perjury. Yet the state continued to lavish large sums of money on them in actions against the police. It is high time it stopped."

The House of Lords was our absolute last stop, and in November 1981 they upheld Denning's judgement. There was nowhere left to go; yet our case would not lie down. By 1980 public figures in Ireland and some investigative journalists were starting to ask questions.

Seven years of travelling back and forth from Birmingham to the Isle of Wight were taking their toll on Eileen. Often she would do the journey in one day; in the summer months she might stay overnight in a bed-and-breakfast. The Home Office paid travelling expenses and minimal allowances for meals, but these didn't stretch far enough most times. A Birmingham-based Conservative MP once described visitors to us in the Isle of Wight as "day trippers," which was deeply offensive to Eileen. In the early days of my imprisonments in Albany she got minimum financial assistance from the Home Office to cover the cost of her fare by coach and ferry to the island and for accommodation in a hostel funded by the Home Office and used for overnight stay by visitors to Albany or Parkhurst. Eileen paid for anything else she required, including hot meals on those long winter days travelling across the midlands to see me. The Isle of Wight may be a day-tripper's pleasure, but there was no pleasure for Eileen on those long journeys from Birmingham.

As time went by we had reasonable visiting conditions, with limited privacy. Nevertheless it was time for a move closer to the midlands for Eileen's sake. I was doing all right in Albany, having established certain rights and privileges not commonly enjoyed by category A prisoners, especially Irish prisoners. At the age of fifty-two, I was the oldest prisoner there. However, I had been in Albany a long time, and a change would be good for me.

I was sent for one day by a Home Office official. "You're looking for a move." "I didn't request it. I shouldn't be here. I'm innocent." "Well," he said, "I don't normally see people in your category, but if you want a move ..." I told him it was becoming harder on my wife and that a move to Long Lartin might be helpful to her.

A few weeks later I got a bang at 6 a.m. "You're on the move." My good mate Fletch heard the call. He jumped up, banged on his cell door to be let out. "Come on," he said, "I want to give him something." I hung about in my cell; I wanted to say goodbye to Fletch. He had been good to me. But they never opened his cell door.

In my foolishness I had made a specific request to be sent to Long Lartin, because I knew it and felt it would be a reasonable prison to be transferred to. However, my mistake was to name a prison, because prisoners never get what they ask for; and I was taken to Gartree in June 1982.

I had survived, to my own amazement, my first seven years of a life sentence.

10

GARTREE PRISON, 1982–1987

On the way up in the category A van, handcuffed to a screw—something I hadn't been for a few years now—I wondered how I would be received. They didn't know me in Gartree and had only my reputation to go on. Over seven years I had successfully broken down most of the prejudices and hatred I experienced when I first went to Albany. The perception of me as a mass murderer had long been dropped by the inmates and the prison authorities—though the latter wouldn't for a second have conceded that point to me. I wondered if I would have to start all over again, renew my battle to get them at least to view me as an ordinary man, if they wouldn't go so far as to believe I might be innocent.

Gartree is another modern prison, set in the countryside outside Market Harborough in Leicestershire. I was my usual apprehensive self as I arrived, though no longer the fearful person who had arrived in Albany seven years earlier. I had lived with people whose ability to survive all kinds of difficulties in prison had taught me a lot, and I had learnt a few tricks about how to protect myself and survive. I had fought some successful battles for my rights in Albany. I now felt able to challenge the screws without agonising about it.

Everyone was banged up when I arrived. The reception screws admitted me in a matter-of-fact way, which was a relief. One of them commented to his colleague, "Christ, this one's on open visits."

The first prisoner I bumped into I knew from Albany. He was very friendly and greeted me with surprise. "Good lord, where have you come from? You look as if you've been in Spain." Later I met a few more blokes I knew in Albany. Most of all that first evening, hearing all the Brummie accents made me realise I was nearer my home.

I met Paddy Hill next morning. He was full of talk and news; he was still corresponding with the world about our case. I was shocked by his appearance, though. He had lost a lot of weight; he was ashen-faced, and looked drawn and stressed. We were on separate wings, so I subsequently didn't see that much of him.

It took a good six months to re-establish a routine for myself in Gartree. Lots of rules and regulations were different. Exercise periods were shorter, which was a killer for me. On the other hand, prison visits were now more frequent and the conditions much better. The rooms were bigger and the space between the visiting tables much wider, giving more privacy, though the screws were never very far away. Eileen was now able to get the prison bus every two weeks, direct to the gate of the prison.

Gartree, like Albany, was an ultra-modern prison with everything electronically controlled. Lights in the cells, cell doors, prison gates, access to public areas of the prison were all electronically directed. If you wanted attention at night you pressed a button. I had grown used to it after being seven years in Albany, but what you never get used to is the hourly check on you at night when you are alone in your cell. I was a light sleeper. The sound of the flaps being raised and dropped I could hear long before they reached my cell. Sometimes if a screw was inconsiderate, or in a bad mood, or if I happened to be in a deep sleep and not moving, the screw would shine the torch right into my face. The shock and annoyance would keep me awake for hours afterwards. The knowledge that I was constantly being observed night and day had a peculiar psychological effect on me. It felt sometimes that I was in a prison within a prison. Throughout the day, screws moved about me with a book to sign, verifying my movements. I often wondered why they had to go as far as this. It was as if the punishment of life imprisonment wasn't enough. I had to endure a kind of psychological torture for as long as I remained in prison. Why should any form of justice seek to secure such revenge?

The rules that restricted the people who could visit category A prisoners still applied nevertheless: all visitors who were not family members had to be vetted, photographed, and approved by the Home Office. One day I overheard inmates discussing discretionary visits from American visitors—one of them had been granted such a visit. I was reminded of the time in Albany when I had asked if I could have a visit from Jean's sister from America. I was told I could have any number of discretionary visits from America, but on further requesting if Jean herself, living in Belfast, could come too, I was turned down flat. Because she lived in the "United Kingdom" she wasn't eligible. I decided I would make enquiries to see if I could get away with it here in Gartree, and I asked the assistant governor what the chances were. I waited weeks for the reply, then got what the prison fraternity call "a result." I couldn't believe my luck. It goes to show you how the rules apply differently in different prisons.

I wrote immediately to the Murphys inviting them to come. Denis couldn't, but Jean and their two lovely daughters came. It was a wonderful visit. The Murphy girls' Belfast accents were a delight to listen to. We talked endlessly about home; I never stopped laughing. I went back to my cell immediately: I didn't want to talk to any inmates, just to go over the visit again in my mind and make the happiness it brought me last a bit longer.

I had long ago stopped going to Mass. My experience of the Catholic priests in the prisons didn't impress me a bit: they saw no distinction that I could perceive between their role and that of any other prison officials. The Gartree chaplain came to see me shortly after I arrived. "I've been sent to see you," he said.

"Not at my request," I told him. "Do you know who I am?"

"Yes, I do." He stood looking at me.

"So you know Paddy Hill then?"

"Yes, indeed I do."

"So you know we're innocent."

He looked a bit weary. "That's what Paddy says. In fact every time I see him he repeats the same words to me."

"Well, if you come and see me regularly I'll say the same to you."

He nodded his head, asked me a few more immaterial questions, and then left. He was all right, but he didn't look as if he would take a stand for fair play if it disturbed the prison authorities.

I had a battle to get back on an outdoor job. In the first few months I was stuck in a workshop. They said it was to give them time to do an assessment on me. What for? Didn't Albany tell them I was okay? I harangued the AG for ages; he finally agreed.

Shortly after I came to Gartree I became friendly with Jimmy Robinson, whose case is known as the Carl Bridgewater case.

The other men wrongly convicted in that case were Michael Hickey, his cousin Vincent Hickey, and Pat Molloy, who died in Gartree. Jimmy was in his mid-forties, had a strong Brummie accent, and was a very funny and friendly man. He was good-looking, and reminded me of James Coburn. We talked a lot and he told me over many hours about his life, which wasn't all on the right side of the law. I had great sympathy with him, and was totally convinced of his innocence, as he was of mine.

Jimmy loved football, and we shared many hours talking over classic matches, and when you got me on that subject I was away. He had had all the hassle we had endured, being moved all the time from one cell to another and from prison to prison. When things started to progress on our case he was sincere in his encouragement and good wishes, though he must have felt it badly. Their case received some public attention, due almost entirely to the efforts of Ann Whelan, Michael's mother, who took up the fight the day her son got sent down, working day and night not just for Michael but for all four of them. Ann's husband, Fred, the solicitor Jim Nicholl, and Paul Foot, a prominent journalist who wrote a book about the case, were Ann's main supporters. Jimmy was shifted eventually to Albany, and he told me later it was hell there. Things had changed a lot since I left. A riot and wholesale destruction afterwards resulted in the prison authorities tightening up all the regulations. I shuddered to think how I would have coped with that. Screws get particularly vindictive after riots, and no prisoner escapes. They can keep up their retaliation for months, sometimes years.

I also met Michael Hickey, the youngest of the Bridgewater people. He was a tense young man who ached inside. He couldn't accept what had happened to him. To be a sensitive soul in prison is hard enough, but to be innocent and have to endure every day the barbarity of prison life is pure hell. That young man really went through the mill, and the screws were awful to him. Michael holds the unenviable record of the longest rooftop protest in an English prison; I think it was almost ninety days. He couldn't have picked a worse time: it was in the depths of a cold winter, with hailstones and gales at night. I couldn't sleep thinking about that young lad. I could see his shadow moving across the skylight; all he had on was a prison duffel coat and his prison clothes. In the early days of his protest inmates would tie sandwiches and a flask of hot soup to a rope and pass it up to him from their cell windows, but after a few days the screws caught them doing it and they were punished severely—for showing some humanity to a fellow human being in mental and physical distress. The authorities thought it wouldn't last long, that the hunger and cold would soon have him come to his senses. But the lad's determination was stronger than any of us gave him credit for. I saw young Michael every day while working on the bin party directly below the rooftop where he was perched. His shouts and calls to us became weaker and weaker. I was deeply disturbed by his presence up there for so long in such bitter weather. One day out of the blue I heard him call very faintly. I called up to him. "What is it? Do you want to come down, lad?" I couldn't hear his response but I knew by his demeanour that he did. I told the assistant governor. Michael was returned to the wing very shortly afterwards. The physical and mental stress he had endured told on his face. But I profoundly admired his gutsy determination.

Eileen had a visit from the probation officer a year or so after my arrival at Gartree. She was told she should prepare herself for the fact that I might do twelve years before I would even be considered for parole, and even then it was likely that I would get a "knock-back"—not only be turned down but told not to apply for another ten years. As soon as I heard about this visit I made an appointment to see the assistant governor. What was all this about? Why bother Eileen with this kind of visit? I was going nowhere at any time without my conviction being quashed. They started on about me not getting political status. "I'm not interested in political status or any other status," I told them. "Through the courts I'll get out, the way I came in. I shouldn't be here."

Some inmates went through hell when their time to be considered for parole was drawing near. They would be required to go before the board of prison visitors, who would have received reports from the screws and from welfare and probation officers. Some went through this ordeal several times in the course of their sentence. During the process they were aware of being constantly observed by the screws, whose power over them in this respect was awesome. It was a kind of blackmail, with the screws forever threatening them and reminding them that they should be careful. I watched with tremendous sympathy inmates getting completely carried away, having convinced themselves they were going to "walk" when the reality was that they were more likely to get a knock-back.

I never gave parole a moment's thought. The only way I wanted to leave prison—and I wanted desperately to leave—was by being released. One of the essential requirements to be considered for parole was "to show remorse." How the hell could I show remorse for a crime I didn't commit? I was called in one time to discuss an "F75," the first step towards parole, and was told, "You've got a six-year knock-back." I couldn't believe it. What were they doing? I never gave the slightest hint I wanted to be considered for parole. "Why are you bothering me with this rubbish? I'll come back in six years time and get another knock-back, and then another. We'll never be paroled. We'll never take it. We want our innocence proved. You'll give me nothing. I'm an innocent man, and the truth will come out some day. Till then don't waste my time with F75s." The governor just sighed in resignation; he had heard that speech so many times before. "I'm only doing my job, Callaghan." I heard no more about it.

My privacy and that of my family were very important to me. I couldn't tolerate the screws or indeed the inmates—except those I was close to, and they were few—asking me questions or intruding in any way. Inmates littered their cells with photographs of their children, their wives, lovers, friends, naked women, pop stars, football heroes, and even pictures of their homes. I never displayed a single picture in Albany or Gartree of Eileen or Geraldine. I regarded that part of my life as totally separate from the prison.

I had a picture I was given in my early days at Albany of a beautiful country scene, showing woods and distant fields. It took me back to the countryside all around Antrim. I would stare at that and imagine myself in a quiet country place somewhere in Ireland. Prisoners who came to my cell always remarked on it—wishing, like me, that they could be there. I would be talking to them and I would notice their eyes fixed on my picture. I took it everywhere with me; it got smaller and smaller as I taped it over and over on umpteen prison walls. Geraldine brought me a little wooden statue from Lourdes, which hung on my wall also. Nothing else was displayed. When I moved cells over the years the picture went everywhere with me, as well as the little statue.

When prisoners wanted to be alone to think, read, listen to music or write they retreated to their cells. It was the only place in prison you could be alone and be private. Many inmates liked to visit others in their cells and entertain. I preferred solitude most of the time. After a whole day of prison life, inmates, and screws, it was essential for me to escape to the privacy of my cell. I always found plenty to occupy me and wrote endlessly, which gave me a lot of satisfaction.

Paddy spent a lot of time in isolation—sometimes at his own request, so that he could concentrate on his writing. He had been in touch with Sir John Farr, Conservative MP for Market Harborough, for some time before I went to Gartree; I wrote and requested a visit after I arrived there. He was by now familiar with our case, and Paddy showed me several copies of letters he had written and responses he had received from the Home Secretary. Farr was a gentleman of the old school of fair-minded English people who gave everyone a hearing. When he came to see me I wasn't sure what to say to him, but he made it clear that he was fighting for the truth and wasn't satisfied with the answers he was getting. I was very impressed by his work; he was a good man. He took the trouble many others didn't who we should have been able to regard as our natural allies, such as the Irish Government and Irish politicians, who only responded to our pleas by stating that though they were "concerned" to see that we had justice they were "powerless" because we were not Irish citizens!

Irish embassy officials appeared after Paddy wrote a letter about them to the *Irish Post*. They showed little awareness of our case when they met us, urging Paddy not to write any more complaining letters—advice I dare say Paddy was not likely to take too seriously.

But Paddy's isolation was by no means always voluntary. Once I was passing by one of the workshops and heard crashing and shouting inside. "Go on, Paddy, let them have it. Good on you, Paddy," then more crashing and banging. Paddy had done a demolition job on several sewing machines, out of sheer frustration. He was owed some wages and the prison was withholding them. Paddy declared that he shouldn't be in prison in the first place and that fighting for a few bob he was entitled to was not on. He promised to make the prison pay for his losses in another way, and he did it in style!

In 1985 Granada Television commissioned Chris Mullin, who later became a Labour MP, to investigate our case for their *World in Action* documentary series. He and a researcher, Charles Tremayne, were to investigate two elements of the case that featured significantly in the trial: the scientific evidence, and our confessions. Granada paid to have the tests Skuse carried out repeated; the Home Office provided the formula used. They got positive results on three nitrocellulose samples: a cigarette packet, a picture postcard, and a wooden surface coated with age-old varnish—these were all things that were handled by the men on the train to Heysham that fateful night. There was also a positive result on a test carried out five minutes after a person handled a pack of playing cards.

Roy Jenkins, the Home Secretary at the time of the explosions, said the results produced a "lurking doubt" about the convictions. For a politician of his stature to come out with this statement was a great leap forward for us. Three days after the programme Skuse was out of a job, having been retired—the Home Office admitted later—on grounds of "limited efficiency."

The Home Office qualified their explanation of Skuse's retirement: his "limited efficiency" was not connected to his work on our case. The Home Secretary, Douglas Hurd, ordered a review of our case.

The governor arranged for Paddy and me to watch the programme together the following day. Paddy asked for it to be videotaped so that the rest of the prisoners could see it. As we watched the programme Paddy smoked like a trooper. "We got the bastards, we got them!" His recorded voice in the programme came as a big surprise to me. I had seen him go over on a visit the week before, where the tape must have been made, but I don't know how he managed to do it. Paddy would chance anything; and that tape recording going out on the programme wouldn't have pleased the governor.

Watching the programme and its revealing of our whole story was an intensely emotional experience. All Paddy's letter writing and endless hours in voluntary isolation were beginning to pay off. Back on Paddy's wing all the prisoners were shouting, "Good on you. You'll be walking soon." Back on my wing it was much the same: prisoners were pleased for us, many shook hands and wished us luck—though I was always conscious of the sad ones, who found it hard to share in our jubilation: they were going nowhere. I sat down that night and wrote to the *Birmingham Post and Mail* restating again my undying belief that the truth would come out in the end.

In addition to his work on the *World in Action* team, Chris was writing a book on our case. Eileen had a powerful memory for detail and was extremely clear in her recollection of events, which helped a great deal. After nearly a decade of hardship and struggle it was amazing to me how easily she could recall things that happened.

Nothing was too much trouble for Chris Mullin. Little did I know when I first met this very confident, educated Englishman that he would turn up such trumps for all of us. He was well briefed and knew a lot about our arrest, the trial, and the assaults in Winson Green, which made it easy to tell him things and to recall events. He had a touch of the detective about him.

There was a breakthrough when Chris Mullin was contacted by a policeman who had been in Queen's Road police station on the night when we were being interrogated. This was as a result of a letter I had written to a Birmingham paper about our case and our innocence. PC Tom Clarke saw my letter and responded. News got around that he was going to blow the lid.

The second programme went out too late and we couldn't see it till the morning, but I had asked a screw just to tell me who the policeman was. At a quarter past ten that night a piece of paper was stuck under my door. *The copper's name is Tom Clarke. PS. The programme was very good.* I couldn't sleep that night.

We watched the programme three times the following evening; it was accurate beyond my wildest dreams. We felt immensely grateful to Tom Clarke for his courage. For a policeman to speak out like that took some guts. The dramatisation of some events made me shudder, especially the interrogations. Blokes shook their heads in amazement, couldn't believe what they heard—the television had powers of persuasion not available to us. They were encouraging. "Won't be long now, Hughie."

I was delighted for Eileen and Geraldine, who could at last hold their heads up. So-called friends who deserted them may have felt some shame when they watched our true story being revealed. I couldn't wait to read what Patsy thought about it and indeed all the people from home who never doubted me even if they were powerless to do anything for me.

The *World in Action* programmes had a profound and immediate effect on many people, young and old, English as well as Irish. We got letters of support, many expressing apologies for what had happened to us, many more outraged and vowing to do what they could. A young lad from Huddersfield wrote me the following letter, which I have always treasured.

Dear Mr Callaghan,

Last night I emptied my money box and I asked my mum to take me to the shop because she could change my money into a £5 note. My mum and dad told me all about you and the other men. I couldn't send all the men money so I am sending it to you because you are the oldest.

PS. My mum and dad have seen you on TV, and I also. We all feel very sorry for what happened to all of you.

Tony.

I wrote back, and he wrote again and told me he showed my letter to all his school mates.

The months after the first programme saw the emergence of a campaign group in London. I received a letter from Paul May, who explained that the group had one objective: "the release and exoneration of the men known as the Birmingham Six." The group's plans included a public meeting with Tony Benn and Robert Kee, both of whom I knew would be very supportive. A leaflet was produced by Paul May outlining our case, then a poster appeared. Billy Power's seventeen-year-old daughter Breda joined the group and spoke at its public meetings, though she looked so young in the newspaper photographs.

We started to get letters from the treasurer, Bob Dawson. Bob's letters were humorous notes with money enclosed—a few bob at first, then a postal order for a hundred pounds. I couldn't believe it. I had never had that much money in one go—ever!

Father Joe Taaffe, who Eileen knew well for some time before the programme, was spearheading the campaign in Birmingham with a wonderful Englishwoman called Anita Richards. She wrote lots of times and was working with others on a quarterly news bulletin. Support groups followed in Nottingham, Newark-upon-Trent, Manchester, and Glasgow. In Dublin a group was established and produced terrific publicity; later they put a weekly picket on the British embassy in Dublin. After our years in the wilderness, I was mesmerised by all this activity.

Eileen told me about Sue Milner, whose work predated all the new groups, but it must have been a great boost to her to find others willing to help and campaign. Eileen was in contact with them all, and travelled with Kate McIlkenny to meetings in Birmingham and later in London.

My practice was not to open my letters until all was quiet at night after final lock-up, then I would read them all and sit down to reply, and sometimes I was still there at one o'clock in the morning. One day I received forty letters. Some people wrote regularly, beautiful letters that didn't just talk about our case but about their families as well. I had many letters from Kathleen Doody, an Irishwoman living in Yorkshire, and another woman called Margaret Szabo in Luton. I also had several letters from Irish people living in London working within the London Campaign. A man from Enniskillen called Felix Maguire often wrote and put in the odd fiver; Seán Healy and Jack Kennedy in London gave very good descriptions of what people in London were doing for us. They would send in copies of leaflets they were distributing or a copy of a programme following a concert or a show. I often wondered what they were like, these people who were so kind and generous in their concern.

The screws were irritated by all the work it created for them. The censors were kept busy, and some of the letters were very forthright in their condemnation of the whole legal establishment, including the prison regime. Prisoners, especially when in category A, were very restricted with regard to who could and couldn't write to them. Screws censoring letters took enormous liberties and often held back letters just to be vindictive if they had it in for you. This holding on to the personal mail of inmates created deep resentment and frustration. Our rights as human beings were constantly violated, without our knowing about it.

On top of that, a prisoner could not refer in any way to prison conditions, nor make any complaint about ill treatment or any other grievance. If a prisoner is troubled about some element of prison life his natural inclination in a letter to his family or those close to him would be to share his worries with them. That basic right is denied to prisoners, and this denial specifically enforced on category A prisoners.

I recall my intense anger over a letter the screws held back when I was in Albany. An assistant governor called me in this particular morning. "I have a letter for you here. It should be okay: her mother writes to you, they know all about you. I don't think you will have problems getting it passed by the Home Office." I responded immediately, already annoyed that the letter was being held back. "I know who the girl is, so why can't I have the letter?" Correcting me, the AG became pedantic. "You know her aunt, but you don't know this girl." "I saw her when she was four years old. Her mother and aunt write to me frequently. Isn't that enough?" My frustration showed on my face. "Well," he said, "that is the situation." I got nowhere.

Later the same day I was given the letter. Looking forward to reading it, I held it till banging-up time that night. I read the date. The letter was three months old. I couldn't believe it. I was absolutely livid and prepared myself for a blazing row with the AG the following morning. The letter was an innocent, sweet letter from a young girl in America called Ann Johnson whose aunt and mother were from home and used to be good friends of mine. The letter was full of nostalgic recollections about me, told to her by older members of her family. She made no reference to my case, or to anything remotely controversial, except to say how sorry she was about everything that happened to me. Having read the date and then the contents of a perfectly innocent, kind letter from a young person, I was very angry that the prison regime could be so callous to any prisoner, but most of all that the screw had lied to me. He never let on that the prison had held the letter for so long. He behaved as if it had just arrived.

I almost yelled at the screw on duty, "What kind of sick people are you?" I reminded him that he once said to me it was more than his job was worth to hold back letters without letting me know. "Did you not also say that if you were to do so you would get me to sign the appropriate form? Your reason for holding back this letter was just a pathetic excuse. There was no form completed, because you knew you would have to provide a reasonable excuse for holding back a letter of this kind from a young girl writing only about domestic matters. Churchill was right. The system is run on lies—maintaining an element of truth. In this case it's just a very tiny element of truth."

"Look, Callaghan, you are lucky to get the letter at all." "Indeed I am," I said. "In fact I am surprised you even bothered to let me know about it. I dare say there is plenty more stuff in my private property you haven't given to me." I was proved right many years later. Upon my release I found that there had been many letters censored and other goods sent to me that were never passed on to me during my imprisonment.

The best coverage of the agitation was in the *Irish Post*, which also printed several excellent editorials analysing our case. Its letters column was dominated by our case. Paddy wrote a brilliant letter to the *Post* complaining about the years of inactivity of the Irish embassy in London and the Irish Government in general. By 1987 we had been in prison almost thirteen years; where had they been all that time? Their subsequent activities on our behalf were all as a result of the exposures by the *World in Action* programmes, Chris Mullin's book, the work of Gareth Peirce, our own efforts—most notably Paddy's persistent letter writing—and latterly the work of campaign groups.

There were some Irish politicians, however, who were different. David Andrews was one of these. He came to see me and Paddy just before the 1987 appeal announcement. He was with a party of four other TDs, but he stood out as being informed and sincere. I liked him from the start. He promised to do what he could to put more pressure on the Irish Government to speak out; I didn't feel he was doing it only out of a sense of duty but that he cared, and there was no doubt in my mind that he believed we were innocent. Other Irish politicians followed his lead and came to see us, including Peter Barry. Senator Pascal Mooney used whatever influence he had to lobby the Irish Government and his own party, but I know he found it hard going. In the early days of our case he told me once it was a "big switch-off," but he doggedly pursued it over the years.

Even from inside prison we sensed that things were happening. The British legal establishment was getting rattled. Chris Mullin was asking embarrassing questions in the House of Commons. Gareth, I knew from Paddy, was at the root of all the success: nothing could have been achieved without her work. Paddy sang her praises constantly.

That Christmas we received cards by the sackful. The screws just didn't know what to make of it all; some clearly resented it. It made me laugh. Is this what you had to endure to become popular? I was delighted with the attention we were getting but it didn't go to my head: we weren't back in the courts yet. The *Daily Telegraph*—of all papers—speculated that our case would be referred but that the Guildford Four would fail. An inmate commented to me, "If that's coming from the Tory press there's some-thing in it: they're in touch with their friends in the government, and they know the score. It's good news, Hughie."

All the agitation worked; Gareth's efforts and Chris Mullin's book forced the Home Secretary to his feet on 20 January 1987. "As the house will be aware, the safety of these convictions has since been challenged, notably in a book by Mr Chris Mullin ... I have examined all the material with great care. I am satisfied that there is new evidence that would justify my referring this case back to the Court of Appeal, and I have now done so." He also announced that as a result of the new evidence he had ordered an enquiry into the conduct of the West Midlands police following our arrest; this enquiry, however, would be undertaken by their colleagues from the Devon and Cornwall police.

I didn't hear the announcement but I learnt about it very quickly. An inmate ran towards me on the stairs, followed by others. They couldn't wait to speak, they were shouting to me as they approached. "Have you heard? Have you heard? You've done it! You're walking!" "What are you on about?" My heart skipped. I had a good idea, but I didn't dare express it in case I was wrong. "You're for the Appeal Court, mate." I could still hear the surprise in my voice. "Christ almighty, where did you hear this?" "On the radio just now." I let out a yelp and ran to my cell and switched on my radio. "The case of the six Irishmen known as the Birmingham Six, convicted in 1975 of the Birmingham pub bomb explosions, is to be sent back to the Court of Appeal ..." It was true. I sat on my bed and savoured the moment alone. After all these years, the truth was coming out at last.

The governor sent for us. He also asked for Paddy Armstrong of the Guildford Four to come down at the same time. I was given a pep talk, and was advised to take the news calmly. "Don't take anything for granted." There were no expressions of surprise at our good fortune, but he was all right. He wasn't hostile, just a bit indifferent. Paddy Armstrong was called in next, just to be told he got a knock-back. How could the governor have been so tactless as to call him down at the same time as us? Paddy was a mild-mannered young Belfast man, always very quiet and without the slightest hint of aggression, despite his years in prison. We all of course viewed the four Guildford people as being in the same position as ourselves, wrongly imprisoned in a massive miscarriage of justice.

I had an excellent solicitor called Stuart Manders, whom Eileen had engaged just before I left Albany. He was a warm-hearted, generous man, efficient as well as caring, well known in the Black Country as a Labour councillor and a civil liberties champion. He also knew the score with George Reade and other West Midlands police officers; their paths crossed several times.

However, Paddy had for a long time believed we should all engage Gareth Peirce; she was based in London, and in the forthcoming appeal that would become essential. I used to see her at visiting time talking to Paddy. One day when I was out on a visit just after the announcement I asked her if she would represent me, and she agreed. I wrote to Mr Manders and thanked him for all his work and kindness. He accepted the decision and understood my need for a London solicitor; Gareth, he considered, was the best we could get.

My first official visit with Gareth was a marvellous experience. She was a great listener. She bought me tea from the tuck shop and spoke to me as if she knew me for years. I knew I had made the right decision. She said she would have a few papers for me to read and comment on; when they came a few weeks later there were reams of it. I couldn't believe it, and I didn't feel I had the confidence to plough through it all; but that was her way: she referred everything back to you for comment. No point was too small to be questioned, gone over, re-examined. I enjoyed doing it and became fairly familiar with the papers after a while. Gareth gave me back my dignity and self-respect. If only, if only she had been around in 1974!

As our appeal date approached, our spirits were up and down. The news from the campaign groups was very encouraging. Eileen's demeanour had changed: she was confident now, felt she could look up and speak out. Our innocence was the talk of the town. Numerous articles were appearing in Irish and British papers. The *Birmingham Post and Mail,* however, was still referring to us as the "Birmingham bombers." I wrote and complained.

The preparation for the appeal took months. Prisoners stopped me all the time, asking when I was going: they thought the appeal meant that our release was a certainty, which of course it wasn't. The establishment made it clear they were fighting back, and the Director of Public Prosecutions would be challenging the appeal. But it was amazing to see the difference in the attitude of the prison authorities: they were more cautious in their relations with me, doing everything by the book. We had the eyes of the press and a large sympathetic public on us, and they were very much aware of that.

News about our case had spread internationally, and the London group were organising to have observers at our appeal. There were congressmen from America, TDs from Ireland, and general secretaries from big British unions. During that summer several unions in Ireland and Britain passed resolutions of support and made generous donations to the campaign. Churchmen such as Cardinal Ó Fiaich, Bishop Edward Daly of Derry and priests from the Irish Chaplaincy who had been active on our behalf for a few years agreed to attend. Father Bobby Gilmore, Director of the Irish Chaplaincy, later became chairman of the National Birmingham Six Campaign. Cardinal Hume was due to send a representative.

Eileen's magnificent efforts can never be forgotten. The McIlkenny daughters supported their father tirelessly and got coverage in the midlands papers. Kate did terrific interviews on television: she just told it to them straight, never flinching. There were numerous letters from Sandra Hunter to everybody important, and in London the Power family were working hard: Breda and her mother, Nora, and Billy's sister Patsy were speaking here, there and everywhere. Thanks to Chris Mullin, MPs by the dozen wrote to me with letters of support and encouragement. Tony Benn spoke at a meeting in Dublin in June.

A screw came to me in my cell round about this time and said, "A bishop wants to see you." I agreed to meet him, and I'm very glad I did. It was Bishop Edward Daly. There were two or three priests with him, and Paddy and I were together on the visit. Paddy did a lot of the talking, and the room was fogbound with smoke. It was a memorable visit. Bishop Daly asked us all about ourselves and our families and about life in prison. He knew my people in Belfast, and we talked about that too. He wasn't like a lot of churchmen I encountered in prison: he was full of compassion, a man you could share your concerns with without feeling you would get the authorities' view rather than the view of a concerned human being.

At the end of the visit we were taken aback when he and the other priests stood up and said that we should part with a prayer. I think both Paddy and I were embarrassed. Praying was something I no longer practised, though I never lost completely my inner faith: I believed in some kind of God, it's just that he hadn't been very good to me over the years. The whole scene made me smile afterwards. Some of the inmates slagged us about it, but I let their remarks go; they could never understand this peculiar element of an Irishman's culture. All the visitors in the room as well as the inmates looked surprised to say the least; but the biggest surprise was expressed on the faces of the screws. They looked so uncomfortable!

Bishop Daly came to visit us a few more times after that, and he used to come on the wing with us. He told me he would be attending the Court of Appeal, and would give evidence on an aspect of our case that seemed to perplex their lordships: why we were on our way to the funeral of a man who had blown himself up.

The visiting-room created its own excitement for us and for

visitors to other inmates. I recall with some pleasure the visitors to two young Welsh miners who were serving long sentences for the accidental killing of a driver when a concre'e block they were using in a protest was thrown onto his car. Their visitors used to take up two tables, gangs of them—half the Welsh mining community, it seemed. They used to come over, shake hands with us, get all excited, giving thumbs-up signs of support. I liked the lads. Whatever they did they appeared to me as two young lads who never looked like notorious murderers: just youngsters caught up in something far bigger than themselves. Their union, the NUM, was in fact the first union to come out in support of us. They gave a lead to other trade unions.

The appeal was due to start on 2 November 1987. A few weeks before this Gareth had put in a request that we all be placed in the same prison. Having had some warning that I was leaving Gartree, I was able to say my goodbyes. Some people believed we were being released. It was hard sometimes to convince them that this was just another stage in our fight back—a very important one, but nevertheless just a stage we had to go through. A young lifer I got along well with, Arthur Nailor, asked me to leave my precious radio. I would love to have done it, but I told him I could be back and I would need it. I hoped I wouldn't, but I wasn't taking any chances.

Our departure from Gartree wasn't at the crack of dawn, as was usual, but in the lazy afternoon. I had a nice suit in Albany but it was stolen; I ended up wearing a sports jacket and trousers. It was a nice feeling to be in civvies again. It's amazing the psychological effect of changing out of prison clothes, even if it's just for a court appearance.

Paddy was already in reception when I arrived. "I gave all

my gear away: a plastic bag full of stuff—everything gone." He was dressed in jeans and a shirt and jumper, and was carrying nothing. "This will do me," he said. He was as high as a kite, and very confident. It would set the adrenalin going just to look at him. Paddy thought we were going to Wormwood Scrubs, because the appeal was in London and Billy and Dick were in the Scrubs, but it wasn't to be. We were taken to Long Lartin prison in Evesham, Worcestershire, in the heart of England. I never returned to Gartree.

11

A NEW APPEAL

No explanation, of course, was given for our move to Long Lartin. The appeal was being heard more than a hundred miles away down in London. Prisoners get used to being kept in the dark: it was standard practice to move category A prisoners at a moment's notice; but under our circumstances it was a bit strange—and even stranger when we learnt that Billy and Dick were being brought up from Wormwood Scrubs in London to Long Lartin. I later heard through the grapevine that no other prison wanted the responsibility of housing all six of us. We were drawing too much public attention, something prison governors don't like.

Long Lartin suited me, because I had been there for a brief spell during the screws' trial and I had found it tolerable. John Walker was in Long Lartin already. He had been there for more than a decade. I was looking forward to meeting him; we had not seen each other since the trial in 1975.

Paddy and I were the first to arrive. The reception screw recognised Paddy immediately. "Long time no see, Hill." Paddy immediately struck up a conversation with the screw. "You're a long time here, guv." "Seven years before my pension now," the screw replied, without looking at either of us. "I bet you'll be glad when that time comes, guv." "I will, I will." The screw then turned to me. "Hello, you were just here for a short spell." I nodded my head in recognition. I always found it hard to be pally with screws, even decent ones.

When they were checking our possessions Paddy commented, "You won't be long searching me, guv. I'm travelling light." He had all he possessed in a small plastic bag. After we were searched we were taken onto the wing, and we could hear the inmates shouting as we approached, "The Six are here! The lads are here for the appeal." Paddy peeped through the spy-hole of John's cell. He was lying on the bed, smiling broadly. "Where's that fella Walker? Get up, you latchico!"

We had to wait for association time before John could come out of his cell. He came over and threw his arms round me. It had been a long time; we were both silver-haired men in our fifties now. He looked lean, athletic-looking, but pale. He wanted everyone to meet us, kept stopping prisoners to introduce his friends. It was clear that he was a king in his castle.

Gerry Hunter, who was transferred from Wakefield prison, was calm and smiling; he hadn't changed a great deal. But it had been very hard on Gerry. His children were infants when he was arrested. For a few moments the four of us stood there looking at each other. We were hardly able to speak to each other after all the years that had passed since we were together, but somehow we got over it.

John wanted to celebrate our arrival, and he invited us to a meal in his cell! There were ten or perhaps eleven people in the cell. Gerry was always a quiet person, not one for celebrations, but he joined in the party. We had a good drink of John's home-made brew and a good laugh. The cell reeked with the smell of food, drink and smoke and ten men packed into a cell designed for one.

Although it was a pleasant reunion, there in the middle of a prison wing, it still felt very strange. People kept coming to the cell to see what we looked like; but what better way to be introduced to one's new residence! We were there for nearly three hours. The screws left us till bang-up time.

Billy and Dick arrived shortly after us. They weren't very happy at being taken all the way from London. It seemed pointless if we all had to go back down again for the appeal; but constant uprooting of category A prisoners was part of what we were forced to endure. Even in our brief moments of joy the authorities would not let us forget our place and our status, though we hardly needed reminding.

There we all were a few days later in the office of the governor, Joe Whitty. He told us he had been asked by the Home Office to house us all till the appeal. It was a pretty liberally run prison, he said, and he hoped we wouldn't take advantage of that. He invited questions. Paddy immediately asked if we would get wages—being on appeal, we were not required to work, and we were "guests" at Long Lartin. Joe Whitty assured us we would enjoy full rights. He advised us against getting drunk. Whitty was okay, and the prison had a good record of providing reasonable opportunities for sport and education.

At a meeting with Gareth Peirce to prepare for the appeal, in March 1987, Billy, Paddy, John and I were introduced to our barristers, Mike Mansfield and Richard Ferguson. We were in great form, and there was a lot of laugh and banter between us in the visiting room. John kept calling Richard Ferguson "sir," and I remember Ferguson saying, "It's all right, John, you can call me Richard." He was a lovely man, with a soft but very recognisable north of Ireland accent. He was a former Unionist member of Stormont—not perhaps someone we would have a lot in common with, but on our first meeting I found him very encouraging. Mike Mansfield appeared very optimistic and talked a lot to Billy and Paddy about the scientific evidence. Both of them were well informed—get Billy onto the subject of forensic scientists and scientific evidence and you couldn't stop him.

Our first meeting with our new barristers was a very encouraging experience. These men were on our side and were keen that we should succeed.

Gareth was cautious about the appeal. She gave us a very good description of the procedures that would be followed in the court. All our legal people were caring, and determined that we should understand fully every stage of the proceedings. The proceedings at Lancaster were a complete shock. This time we would be prepared.

Gareth told us she'd be sending us some papers to read. A few weeks later boxes and boxes of papers arrived for us. There was a note from Gareth: "Study the papers very closely and take notes." I wondered if I could go through it all, there was so much of it. It was definitely going to keep us busy until the appeal, due to start in November. Gareth came regularly, and there were always more papers to read. Billy and Paddy were very good at it and knew the minutest details of the evidence. I kept notes of everything I read and made comments beside the points I wanted to raise with Gareth. She inspired us to work for our own benefit; when someone shows that much consideration and belief in your innocence you want to respond by doing your best to help. That's how I felt: she motivated us as no other person had succeeded in doing before.

During the months coming nearer to the appeal we were

receiving information about the enquiries being conducted by the Devon and Cornwall police. Tom Clarke had been interviewed for several hours; they took statements involving his private life, which seemed to me unnecessary. I remember Gareth saying several times that we were waiting for papers from the Devon and Cornwall police. They were investigating other police officers, and it all took time.

During the preparation period we had a lot of unnecessary aggro from the screws as well as from the sheer inefficiency of some of the prison routine. We were kept waiting for visits long after our visitors had arrived; we were cut short on our time on a visit, and that's the worst thing you can do to someone in prison. I had a poster stuck inside my door with a big slogan, *Free the Birmingham Six*. I knew it got up the noses of some of the screws, as did all the activity on our behalf in the media and by our defence people. Billy and Dick complained about the visiting shambles and their general dissatisfaction with the prison's imposition of rules, and in the end asked for a transfer back to the Scrubs, which was eventually granted.

If you were a category A prisoner expecting a visit you had to wait on the wing of the prison till a screw was ready to escort you over at each point along the way. All other categories of prisoners made their own way over to the centre unescorted. While they were allowed in to their visit, we were forced to hang about waiting for available screws and dog-handlers. Yet we could go to the prison hospital, the canteen and along the passages of the prison on our own. Why couldn't we go over to the visits unaccompanied? We were repeatedly late seeing our visitors. It was frustrating for them and for us. They didn't add time on to the visit to compensate either. By the time I got to see my visitors I was thoroughly fed up. It undoubtedly took a lot of the satisfaction out of the visit. You might spend the first few minutes complaining about being kept waiting, starting your visit on a down note, which didn't help.

I complained to Joe Whitty one day about the treatment of 'A' men on visits. I felt I was speaking on behalf of all the 'A' men on my wing. Our treatment in every respect was shabby, but the visiting situation was out of hand. The screws didn't care if we lost precious time on a visit. We had the same allotted time for visits as non-A men, yet we were put through a whole performance of security before we got to see our visitors. Eileen frequently waited an hour for me to appear.

Later, out on the exercise yard, Whitty came over to me, "Look, I am meeting officials of the Home Office. I am going to call a meeting of all 'A' men before I go. We can go through their concerns and you can raise the visiting situation again." Back on the exercise yard weeks later, Whitty said to me, "Look Callaghan, I am seeing to all this. The procedures will change; they will improve." Joe Whitty was an exceptionally flexible, intelligent governor who listened. Normally you would climb a mountain quicker than see a governor. Joe Whitty was accessible to the prisoners and frequently walked around the yard with them. This episode demonstrated for me that if you challenged the system directly you could get a response, providing you had reasonable governors.

As the appeal drew closer my nerves were on edge, and the slightest problem or the slightest bit of aggro made me want to explode. I was so tense I spent time in the hospital wing, supposedly getting away from it all, but there were so many others with severe illnesses of a mental kind that it was no rest, no escape. Even there the screws were noisy and harsh, with nothing gentle or caring about them; we might as well have been stuffed dummies in the beds. The prison wings were homely by comparison; I was relieved to go back to the peace of my cell.

While waiting in Long Lartin for our appeal I received news of the death of my brother Tom. I was devastated. We were once very close; in my youth Tom was my hero. The tragedy of the years in between had separated us, but I thought back on the good times we had together, when we travelled all over Ireland and England pursuing one of the shared loves of our life, listening to the pipe bands playing in competitions and exhibitions. With his death a happy part of my life was gone.

When prisoners have news of a death they naturally retreat into themselves. Screws generally know it's best to keep away for a few days, unless, as is sometimes the case, they are particularly crude and brutal, and then the hurt and aching that prisoners feel at this time can be made much worse. It becomes essential to control your emotions in prison, otherwise you don't survive. After Tom's death, prisoners who were mates of mine were very considerate. One good friend, Cyril Birkett, offered me comfort and kind words. Another inmate suggested I might even like a "joint"—anything that might help take away the sadness that you feel at this time. But for me there was only one way to deal with the loss and grief, and that was to live through it in the privacy of my cell.

Joe Whitty allowed me to phone Tom's wife, Mary, and to go to the funeral if I wished. Under the circumstances he said he didn't need to seek the permission of the Home Office: it was at his discretion. He warned me, though, that the media attention on us was at its height and that they could turn Tom's funeral into something obscene—a circus, he thought. He gave me good advice, and he was genuinely concerned for me. I remembered the experience Paddy had when he went to visit his dying father in hospital: he had to remain handcuffed to a screw even while he stood at his father's bedside. It's a harrowing enough experience without enduring such degradation and insensitivity. I spoke to Mary on the phone, and decided after that not to go.

Patsy sent me in some of Tom's more precious possessions, which Mary had passed on to her: his ring, and some photographs of him in his pipe band uniform holding the pipes. They were lovely mementoes to have near me in the cell.

It was a bad time all round for me, thinking about Tom and the appeal and all the media coverage. The tension within me was acute sometimes; but somehow you learn to cope with everything in the end. There's no alternative.

I remained in Long Lartin for nine months, but I didn't see an awful lot of the others, except when Gareth came to visit and discuss matters with us. I got on well with John, though he had his own group of friends and knew the run of the prison. Gerry was on another wing. He and Dick also had different people representing them.

Gareth's legal staff, and a young man, Nick Brown, training to be a barrister with Gerry's solicitor, Ivan Geffen, were still ploughing through thousands of documents sent by the Devon and Cornwall police. Almost on the eve of the appeal, among all the documents, our defence stumbled on a chart detailing the times of interviews, by whom we were interviewed, and where the interviews took place. Superintendant George Reade, who led the investigations, was responsible for drawing up the chart, which was later referred to as the "Reade schedule."

Although the Devon and Cornwall police did not specifically

draw the document to the attention of our defence people, or reveal its existence, it was nevertheless to prove a significant find. At our trial there were numerous contradictions between our account and the police's account of what took place during those interviews immediately after our arrest. This document could help greatly to clear up the discrepancies. Our defence were delighted with their discovery.

As the date approached, the material was still being read and reread by Gareth and her dedicated staff. I was finding it more and more difficult to concentrate. To be perfectly frank, reading the day's horse races or what was happening on the dog track provided a pleasant escape. Gareth was infinitely patient and never pressed us beyond our capabilities. It got on our nerves sometimes when well-meaning prisoners would say, "You're not gone yet, then?" Others knew the score but were so convinced of our innocence that they took it for granted we would win our appeal.

Shortly before the hearing I had a visit from a Dr Gudjonsson to do a psychological report on me at Gareth's request. As I understood it, the purpose was to consider why I might have confessed to crimes I did not commit. I was very apprehensive. My previous experiences of psychologists left me humiliated and demoralised. Psychological tests carried out in prison tend to be viewed—perhaps in ignorance—with suspicion. Dr Gudjonsson eased those concerns from me almost as soon as the interview started.

I was as honest as I was able to be—and the conclusions in the report were not always flattering! "Mr Callaghan's exceptionally high suggestibility and compliance, in conjunction with a nervous disposition and a very timid and submissive temperament, strongly indicate that he is very susceptible to providing erroneous information when placed under pressure ... Mr Callaghan's specific vulnerabilities very likely existed at the time of his arrest in 1974. This is consistent with his own retrospective account of his behaviour and personality ... I believe that it is almost certain that Mr Callaghan possessed in 1974 some vulnerable qualities which seriously impaired his ability to give a voluntary and a reliable statement when interviewed by the police in 1974."

The report was sympathetic, but needed to be received by judges and the opposition with some grace and a desire to understand what made me sign those confessions. As far as I was concerned it was fair and accurate. Gareth was pleased with it, and wrote to me at the time to say she thought it would be very helpful.

In October 1987 we were transferred to Wormwood Scrubs in London, Billy and Dick's abode. The Scrubs was an old prison, very overcrowded, with none of the space or facilities of Gartree or Long Lartin. The cell had no windows; it was a pitch-black hole like a dungeon until the light was switched on. Out in the exercise yard you walked round and round in circles, seeing only the high wall of the prison, with not a blade of grass or a tree in sight and with the screws staying in close proximity. The walls were covered in pigeons' mess. It was winter, and very cold. I got my exercise, but as we were not permanent prisoners no overcoats were issued to us. Basic things were not available; clothes were old and tatty; you couldn't shower in peace; the food was poor; but more than anything else it was a noisy, overcrowded prison that did little to soothe a person's nerves before an important event like our appeal.

Billy was very well liked in the Scrubs. He was a decent bloke and looked out for us, introducing me to people who were very helpful. There was hardly a prisoner who didn't know him. The authorities appeared to have a high regard for him also. I met Father Hugh Sinclair, the Catholic chaplain; he made us all welcome and spoke with great warmth in his voice, and he had a good sense of humour too. He and Billy seemed like mates more than prisoner and chaplain. He was the first prison chaplain I encountered in thirteen years who showed me what a real priest could be like. All prison chaplains were employed directly by the Home Office. They were viewed in the main by prisoners as no different from any others of the prison staff. They contributed with the whole prison regime to your oppression. Hugh Sinclair was so very different in his relations with prisoners and above all else showed great humanity.

Dick was well established there too and was always engaged in activities with other prisoners. He kept his mind active and was interested in self-help groups and the whole range of activities that the Scrubs offered. I was the opposite, I suppose: I wanted only to exercise or to be quiet in my cell, writing or just listening to the radio. It was good to see both Billy and Dick so highly regarded; it was evident that most of the officials believed them to be innocent.

Another psychologist, Dr McKeith, came to visit me twice during October. The interviews were very long, lasting nearly three hours. I knew for a few days beforehand that he was coming, and despite reassurances from Gareth about him I was still fretting about it and found it difficult to concentrate and work out what I would say. Dr McKeith's report, like that of Dr Gudjonsson, was to assess my state of mind at the time of my arrest. His report was detailed, though not entirely comprehensible to a lay person like me; however, as far as I could follow his analysis of me I recognised much of what he said. I only regretted that a person like him was not around in 1974! I believe, though, that even if they were around at the time, such was the determination of society, led by the media, to convict us that their reports would have been treated with disdain.

Gareth expressed herself well pleased with Dr McKeith's work; it remained to be seen what good would come of it. In fact the psychologists' reports were never used. Our legal people took the view that they would be received with hostility and be disregarded by the judges.

Our families were being interviewed regularly in the press and on radio and television. Paddy McIlkenny, Dick's brother, spoke with great authority and conviction, a terrific spokesman for the families. Young Breda Power spoke well too and was a favourite of the media. Some papers were more intelligent and sympathetic in their coverage than others. Some of the cruder tabloid papers still referred to us as the "bombers," but the more serious newspapers were at last giving our story a proper analysis.

It wasn't always easy for journalists. Gerry Hunt, who wrote for the *Birmingham Post and Mail*, took some stick for the articles he wrote about us, and not everyone in his paper was sympathetic. I thought he had a lot of courage to keep going.

On the day before the appeal, a Sunday, Mass was said by Father Hugh. The prison church was packed, and I suppose it was the first time for a long while that the Mass meant something to me. I actually prayed for a good appeal, for things to go reasonably well. There was a powerful sense through Father Hugh's Mass that people throughout the prison wished us well. Even some of the screws wished us luck.

The atmosphere in the Scrubs that night was electric. The whole prison was affected by the excitement and activity our presence generated. There was so much speculation about the possible successful outcome of the appeal that it was difficult not to get carried away. I thought we had a fifty-fifty chance; and considering the fact that few people ever succeeded on appeal, they weren't bad odds.

The appeal began on 2 November 1987. I was up hours before we were called. We were all a bit shaky and keyed up when they came to take us to the Central Criminal Court—the "Old Bailey"—in the heart of London; it was evident that none of us had slept a wink. We were placed in category A vans with police escorts in bikes and cars before and behind, and we were handcuffed. The screws in the vans were fairly mute, but the court police were positively hostile. We were taken straight down to the cells, three to a cell, and they were very cold, damp, and smelly. The food was sparse and horrible. But we were still smiling and talking away to each other. We weren't on trial this time—the system that condemned us was.

Just before we went up to the court our entire defence team came down: Mike Mansfield, looking very different in his wig, Richard Ferguson, Lord Tony Gifford and Ivan Geffen (Gerry's solicitor), and Gareth. There was a lot of shaking of hands and nervous smiles. Tony Gifford moved from one to the next with encouraging words; he was so kind and sincere in his good wishes to me that it is a moment I will always remember. Gareth went round, as quiet-spoken as ever, asking us if we were all right. My stomach was churning but I was coping. The care and concern expressed by those responsible for presenting our appeal couldn't have been better. It was a privilege to have them represent us.

Minutes before we were due to go up to the court, Dick took out a Bible and called for our attention. "These people have a very difficult task ahead of them." He invited us to say a prayer, which we did. Tony Gifford turned and said, "That was very nice, Richard."

Our cold reception by the police and officials was in marked contrast to the one we received when we entered the court. We all looked up at the visitors' gallery, waving and blowing kisses to family and friends. If they'd have got away with it I'd say our families and supporters would have applauded as we entered, but the voice of the law intervened, "All rise," and the judges made their familiar grand entrance.

The relatives were issued with a limited number of tickets, and had to take turns with the seats. Eileen was due down later in the week to take over from Patsy, who now sat quietly in the back of the gallery.

It had been intended that our appeal would be heard in the Royal Courts of Justice in the Strand, which had a much smaller seating capacity for the public. The numerous requests from observers to attend the court led to the authorities having to change the venue at the last minute. In securing so many observers to come and watch British justice on trial the campaign organisers had done a marvellous job—much to the disquiet of the court police. I recognised David Andrews, Peter Barry, Bishop Edward Daly, and Chris Mullin, and there were American congressmen too and representatives from Amnesty International. It was a "full house."

The Lord Chief Justice, Lord Lane, with Lord Justice O'Connor and Lord Justice Brown, presided over the appeal. The Crown was represented by Igor Judge, who had prosecuted in the Carl Bridgewater case, for which three innocent men are still serving life imprisonment. Stephen Brown was a barrister in Birmingham at the time of the bombings, and he would have his memories;

and Lord Lane had the reputation of rarely conceding an appeal.

Some lay people find court proceedings enthralling and enjoy the drama of it all. I don't. My previous experiences in court had a long-lasting effect. We were not in the dock now; but I had mixed feelings about the prospect of sitting in court for several weeks listening to the whole saga again. The press might have changed their attitude, but the judges wouldn't necessarily have. We were, however, more prepared, and our defence team would make sure we understood the proceedings.

There were some parts of the appeal I was looking forward to. We knew from our months of discussions that every detail of how our confessions were obtained and their contents had been examined over and over again. Our team were not only thoroughly familiar with the confessions and all the scientific evidence but, equally important, knew us all well. It was generally accepted, even by media hacks, that we now had the best legal people in England on our side. Our version of events would be presented as never before, and by a defence team who believed us and were totally on our side.

The two former police constables Joyce Lynas and Tom Clarke were due to appear. We were all keen to hear them, feeling immensely grateful for their co-operation.

In his opening speech Lord Gifford outlined the manner of our arrest, the circumstances under which the police had obtained our confessions, and the flawed scientific evidence. He posed the question "whether among the many victims of the Birmingham pub bombings, the dead, the injured, and the bereaved, may not be counted these six men, who would have spent thirteen years behind bars as innocent men while those truly guilty would have gone free. If that is so, the miscarriage of justice will have been one of the gravest in recent times."

I had always conceded that I wasn't physically beaten to the same degree as the others. Nevertheless the interrogation I received for almost three days and nights, deprived of sleep, receiving no food, interrogated by bullies with barking dogs, had all contributed to my signing a false confession. These facts were more eloquently put than I have described them; however, the judge intervened. "He did not complain, did he, of physical injury?" "Very little, my lords." "Just one slap in the face?" It was a small but significant intervention, which sent out clear messages.

The presentation of the "Reade schedule" followed, and Superintendent George Reade took the stand. He replied to questions about the apparent discrepancies in the schedule that appeared not to accord with our recollection of events. The reactions and comments of the judges while this evidence was being considered left us with no illusions. If we were to be believed, we would have one almighty struggle to overcome their scepticism.

The six witnesses we had were not people in positions of power and influence, but their evidence was all we had to go on. There were a cleaner, two prison officers, and three former police officers. A former station cleaner told the court that he found bloodstains where we had been held. Evidence was also heard about our being marked, looking very frightened, being shouted at, pushed and shoved, and prevented from sleeping. Two prison officers from Winson Green gave evidence of receiving us into custody appearing badly bruised and beaten. A chemist who delivered material to Skuse contradicted the Reade schedule on a crucial question of timing.

The first of the two police witnesses to give evidence was Joyce Lynas. It took great courage to stand up to the cross-examination. She was on duty at Queen's Road police station during the time we were being interrogated. She described our appearance, and said we were being treated roughly and subjected to a lot of verbal abuse. We had looked awful; some of us had no shoes on. She acknowledged under cross-examination that she didn't actually see us being beaten. She worked on the station switchboard, not far away from the interrogation rooms, and the banging, shouting and screaming she heard was sufficient to distract her to the point where she couldn't answer some of the phone calls. She was also in and out of the interrogation rooms, bringing tea to the policemen; yet when she was asked by Richard Ferguson if she saw any marks or signs of injury on us she said no. She described us only as looking very rough and tired. We were puzzled.

But Mrs Lynas was having her own problems, which we discovered when she asked to come back five days later to the witness box. She explained that her earlier account wasn't the whole story but that because of the threats to her and her children she didn't tell all. She told the court that before coming to give evidence at our appeal she had received phone calls from people who threatened her and her children if she "squealed" on her former colleagues. After thinking it over she had contacted Gareth Peirce and decided to speak out. She told the court that she saw one of us being assaulted, kneed in the groin. She couldn't describe which one of us it was; but it was a huge step forward. Igor Judge set out to demolish Joyce Lynas, and went over all her previous evidence. We had to listen while this woman was put through the mill, humiliated, because she was honest and courageous and did what none of the others were ever prepared to do, and that was to speak the truth. I felt very sorry for Mrs Lynas, but immensely grateful at the same time.

We were still in the first week of the trial when a bomb exploded in Enniskillen, killing several people attending a memorial service for the dead of the two world wars. The papers were full of condemnation, understandably, of the IRA and terrorists. Sympathetic and substantial coverage of our appeal was very important, and it was essential that the judges know they were being observed. The death of so many in such a horrific way could well have turned the tables against us.

Half way through the second week I became ill and had to be taken to hospital. It was the first time since my arrest that I had set foot in civvy street, and did the police and screws make a meal of it! When I arrived at the hospital they checked every room, cleared patients out of the wards and waiting rooms, and brought in dogs to check the lifts and common areas. They treated the outpatients to a demonstration of the police in action during a "security alert." Throughout all this I remained a few paces behind, handcuffed to a screw. I was scanned lying on my back, still handcuffed to the screw. I believe if I had passed away they would have kept the handcuffs on until I ceased to breathe.

The tests revealed a virus infection, and I remained away from the court on doctors' advice for a few days. I followed the proceedings from my prison bed. The *Irish Times* team, led by Nuala Ó Faoláin, was excellent, with word-for-word coverage the following day. In the prison I read the *Independent*, as well as some of the rags, which reported briefly on the trial; but the *Irish Times* was the only paper to report the hearing verbatim. I believe even the judges asked for the *Irish Times* during the appeal.

After a few days in the Scrubs I was glad to get back to the court and join the others, though things weren't going well for us. I was there to hear ex-Constable Tom Clarke give his evidence. He looked smart but nervous, very different from his television appearance. We all knew this was going to be an ordeal for him; we had read the Devon and Cornwall police papers on him. Some of the witnesses, including fellow police officers, gave the Devon and Cornwall police evidence that was almost entirely derogatory and alleged that he had stolen five pounds from a prisoner. He had been a policeman for twenty-three years until he was dismissed. Looking at him and seeing his willingness to put himself on the line on our behalf I knew I would believe him a damn sight quicker than I would his accusers. The gutter press weren't too kind to him either. I thought he was a brave soul.

Constable Clarke had been at Queen's Road police station on the night we were being put through the mill. When interviewed for *World in Action* he described how he saw a gun being held to a flap on one of the cell doors. He also said there were dogs at the station and that they barked continuously; one of his colleagues told him they had instructions to keep the suspects awake. When questioned he gave the same evidence, though this time he wasn't half so self-assured; and under such conditions, facing Igor Judge, whose sole objective was to demolish his evidence, it wasn't surprising that he faltered. Nevertheless the truth was there if the judges wanted to hear it.

Bishop Edward Daly gave his evidence, explaining why some of us were on our way to the funeral of a man who had blown himself up. He set out to explain the cultural background of the Catholic community in the north of Ireland, how we would go to the funeral of a person like Jamesie McDade, disregarding the manner of his death or how he might have lived his life. He gave an explanation that an intelligent person knowing nothing about Ireland and its people, in fact the most culturally ignorant person, would understand; but it seemed to me from the demeanour of the judges that it was falling on deaf ears.

The former Home Office forensic scientist Dr Frank Skuse, dismissed from his job for "limited efficiency," gave his evidence, which alleged that Billy and Paddy had been in contact with explosives. However, Dr Brian Caddy, head of the Forensic Science Unit at Strathclyde University, and David Baldock, a former Home Office senior scientific officer, had shown that a similar result could be obtained from a wide range of everyday substances, including playing cards, a cleaning material used in bars and on trains, meat pies, and even cigarette smoke. Using more advanced tests, they had failed to find any traces of nitroglycerine, nor were there any traces found on Paddy or Billy's clothes. Skuse took the witness box to be questioned about his methods and his tests. He was a clever and experienced witness, obviously well used to court appearances. He conceded minor things, like his tendency to be sloppy and careless while conducting his tests; for example, it was not his practice to sterilise the containers in which he placed swabs taken from suspects, and he did not always wear gloves; but on more important questions he couldn't be penetrated. For thirteen years it had not been possible for the Home Office to obtain a written description of the methods he had used. He now told the court that he had given the two *World in Action* scientists the wrong formula for their tests. But the two scientists stood by their findings, and said that in their judgement Dr Skuse had indeed given them the right formula.

The scientific evidence was difficult to follow; but their

lordships were very accommodating and patient with Skuse. After the failure to break him, even though his methods were thoroughly discredited, few reporters covering the appeal were expecting us to succeed. We became daily more despondent.

Every day we brought our possessions to the court, just in case we were released, and every day for twenty-eight days we brought them back again. The appeal ended on the eighth of December; and that night we learnt that the verdict wouldn't be given until January. I remember thinking, Why can't they give us the result now? Everyone knows we're going to get a knock-back. What was the point of waiting? I wondered why the judge wanted to wait until after Christmas. What about our agonising wait over Christmas? Our lawyers were very kind and considerate as we departed, and wished us well over Christmas, which they knew would be a difficult time.

Gerry, John and I were taken back to Long Lartin to await the verdict. Paddy was taken to Gartree, and Billy and Dick remained in Wormwood Scrubs.

There was a pleasant surprise for John and me on our return. I went into the room where we picked up our mail and asked if there was anything for me. The screw pointed to big bundles of Christmas cards wrapped in rubber bands. "That's it." "What, for me?" "Yes; and the other lot is for Walker." There were hundreds of them! I just laughed my head off. There was also an envelope from Bob Dawson with a hundred pounds. It was unbelievable how kind people were. It took hours at night to read all the cards, which came from all over the world. I felt that no matter what the verdict was, with this level of support we were coming out; if it wasn't this time it would be another appeal. The outcry against our conviction as expressed in those Christmas cards was too big for the Home Office to continue to resist.

There were cards from Belfast people I hadn't heard from for years. Each one brought back memories and filled me with nostalgia. Some came from old friends, like Mary Mallon, who had been writing to me for years, and Kathleen Doody in Yorkshire, who had written to me almost since my days on remand; she sent a beautiful card and a letter full of hope. Sister Sarah, who never forgot any of us, wrote a lovely letter, full of encouragement and fight. She had applied to visit us, but her request was turned down.

Coming up to Christmas, prisoners do what everyone else does: they write Christmas cards, and if they have a few bob they try to arrange to buy gifts for their loved ones. The screws were unsympathetic to our requests to get cards sent out. "Too late, mate." I was livid. "Can't a man even send out a Christmas card to his wife and daughter?" I complained to Joe Whitty, who always rose above petty practices; I was able to get them out the same day. Christmas is a hard time in prison, and writing Christmas cards was one of the few pleasures. Screws are never the most sensitive of folk at any time of year. It was hard at times like that to imagine that many of them had families of their own.

Gareth called to see us on Christmas Eve. It was a great surprise, and a most pleasant visit. She brought us lots of sweets and goodies. It was a quick visit, but the talk was all easy, no legal stuff now. Gareth was a true friend. What solicitor would have travelled a hundred miles to see a client on Christmas Eve? It took a very special person to do that. Her husband had to wait outside in the car: he hadn't got a visiting order.

A good mate of mine, Mickey Turner, who had travelled down with us in the van when we were going to the appeal and was due to return to Long Lartin before us, promised he would arrange a Christmas turkey for us before we got back. He was true to his word. John, the guy who cooked the meal for us and I enjoyed a traditional Christmas dinner in John's cell. It was as pleasant a way to spend Christmas as we could have made it under the circumstances. Christmas is emotionally very difficult to handle in prison, especially for inmates who have children, and most are relieved to see the end of it.

New Year's Eve brings a different atmosphere. Some inmates would get into great form—it might be their year to be released; for others it was terrible, and you could see men becoming deeply depressed, almost suicidal. We were going nowhere, but somehow that New Year's Eve I didn't feel depressed. The strength to carry on came from the knowledge that there were so many people outside, from all walks of life, who believed in our innocence.

In the second week of January, John, Gerry and I were taken back to the Scrubs for the verdict. As we were going across the reception area of Long Lartin all the inmates were shouting over at us, wishing us well. In the Scrubs we met Billy, Dick and Paddy again, and there was more outpouring of good wishes from the inmates there. I was placed in a cell next to Winston Silcott, one of the Tottenham Three. He was a giant of a man and a very nice guy. The next day he passed me in a paper and wished me luck.

On the eve of the verdict, a Sunday, Father Hugh Sinclair asked me to attend Mass, and I agreed. Dick read the lesson. The church was packed; I had never seen anything like it in other prisons. Remand prisoners came over and wished us well, and Sister Agnes shook hands with all of us, expressing hope for a successful outcome.

That Sunday night was a long night. We were all very nervous. A man has hope right up to the end, but we had been here before, and there were no illusions. If we won this it would be a miracle.

1 2

BACK TO PRISON

On 28 January 1988 we were all back in the Old Bailey to hear the outcome of our appeal. Waiting in the basement cells to go before their lordships, I felt no more than a glimmer of hope. None of us had much to say, each of us occupied with his own thoughts. Dick must have smoked twenty cigarettes, pacing up and down the room. It was the first time in a long while I saw Paddy at a loss for words. Billy looked the most calm, almost philosophically steeling himself for the worst. Gerry and John sat pensively waiting. I had resigned myself to bad news, but you always hoped you might be wrong.

A screw put his head in the door. "Are you ready?" We all stood up and made our way up the same five or six flights of stairs, a journey we had made many times before. Usually one of us would crack a joke or say something, but this time we were six silent men. This was the end of the road.

The court was packed. Gareth looked over at us several times. You felt that if it was a "knock-back" it would be as heartbreaking for her as for any of us. All the work, all the long hours put in to win this appeal could in the next few hours be cast aside by three judges.

Their lordships took their seats, with the attendants puffing up their cushions and making sure they were comfortable in their high chairs. For six hours they took it in turns to read their judgement, from 10 a.m. till 4 p.m. After a while their voices just became a monotonous drone. Their expressions were grave and cold; I could hardly bear to look at them. There was something inhuman in the way they sat there, dressed in wigs and gowns and barely moving any part of their bodies. As they read on, the atmosphere grew more and more tense. They had nothing but bad news to relate to the assembled court.

All six of us sat there in complete silence. Every now and then you could hear sighs of disbelief as the judges rubbished our witnesses one after the other. Mike Mansfield's head hung down for the first time ever. Tony Gifford sat motionless, staring straight at the judges. The press were the only people making noise, walking in and out of the court. You could see they were keen to file their big story, but at the same time hesitating, not wanting to miss the sensational bits. I looked up at the gallery several times. The women in the front row, leaning right over the side trying to hear the judges, still were able to give the odd smile and a defiant wave down at us. Our families were brave and proud people.

All our witnesses were branded as liars, or at best mistaken in their evidence. The brave Joyce Lynas, who returned to the court to tell the truth that most of her former colleagues wanted suppressed, was "a witness who was not worthy of belief." Tom Clarke was nothing more than a man who was out to make money and blacken the name of the West Midlands police. "The conclusion is unavoidable that Thomas Clarke has invented his story about guns and the prisoners standing up and sitting down every fifteen minutes. He has invented the injuries to

Callaghan ... Mr Clarke was a most unconvincing witness ... He is also an embittered man." Another policeman who said he saw six men standing to attention and facing a wall had a mind that played tricks on him, said the learned judges. The two prison officers who said we were already injured when we arrived at Winson Green were "trying to conceal or minimise the part played by the prison staff and the prison inmates in the violence carried out in Winson Green." George Reade was, the judges concluded, "not a person who would have been capable of organising or carrying out such a huge and complicated conspiracy." So many years had passed since the Reade schedule was drawn up that there was bound to be "some measure of confusion in his recollection." It was inconceivable that it was a blueprint for perjury.

When it came to their considerations of Skuse's evidence, their points were endless, and most of it comprehensible to just a few people in the court. They admitted, among other things, to "grave doubt as to the nature of the methods for testing used by Dr Skuse." They didn't, however, regard the scientific evidence as evidence on which the safety of the convictions hung—in contrast to Mr Justice Bridge, who, at our trial, regarded the scientific evidence as crucial.

Lord Lane ended their deliberations by virtually complaining about the Home Secretary sending the case back to appeal in the first place and wasting their lordships' time. "As has happened before in references by the Home Secretary to this court ... the longer this hearing has gone on the more convinced this court has become that the verdict of the jury was correct ... We have no doubt that these convictions are both safe and satisfactory."

The judges delivered their blow with what seemed to us

incredible arrogance. We were small, unimportant people, and by God we felt it. They had an expression on their faces that appeared to suggest they would like to have said, "How dare you approach us?" But even small people have a right to justice. Though it was immaterial now, I barely heard Lane say the words that sent us back behind bars. His voice rose just above a whisper: "The appeals are dismissed."

You could see that the people in the gallery took some time to realise that it was all over. Then I heard a few cries and a voice saying clearly, "It's disgusting. They're innocent." Someone shouted, "They'll be back!"

I looked over at Mike Mansfield and Tony Gifford. What must they have thought of their fellow-professionals. It seems that the mighty must find it hard to concede that they are capable of making mistakes. Gareth sat for a few moments in her seat. She was as calm as ever, but so sad as she approached us. None of us said a word. There were no gestures, no demonstrations. Paddy shook his head, devastated, almost in tears. We had known this might be the result; nevertheless when it was confirmed in such a cruel, dismissive way it was difficult to stand there and take it without crying out. The humiliation was as bad as the rejection.

Even some hardbitten press people who expected the decision were not prepared for the absolute rejection we received. Chris Mullin looked angry; I knew it wouldn't be long before he would lash out at the judges to the press waiting outside. Chris was a mild-mannered person but with the most powerful tongue, and he could condemn injustice with gusto. None of the mighty would escape his wrath.

When we were convicted and sentenced to life in prison, I had no reserves, physical or mental, with which to cope. At that time they could have said or done with me whatever they wished. The whole of British society, led by the media, endorsed our convictions; a life sentence was the least that could have been imposed upon us—that was the commonly held view. This time my mental state was very different. Though I was still devastated by this rejection, I felt a lot stronger mentally. They could continue to imprison my body, but never again could they imprison my spirit. Every morning for the past fifteen years I had faced a challenge, and that was to stay alive, and to fight—fight to the end of my days if necessary to prove my innocence. This was a set-back, a big one; but I was mentally strong enough to take it without collapsing emotionally. Escorted by the screws, we left the court with our heads up.

Back in the cells we put in a request to see members of our families before we were removed again to prison; and while we were waiting we stood around the room in little groups, comforting each other. There were lots of tears as well as encouraging words about the future. Angela Murphy, who worked for Gareth for many years and whom we all got to know well, came in in floods of tears. Paddy was able to crack a joke that made Ivan Geffen laugh heartily; Ivan remarked that he was amazed how well we were able to take this awful knock-back. Richard Ferguson came over to me and said gently, "Sorry about that, Hughie." "Don't be sorry," I said. "We'll be back." But at the end of the day we were lost for words.

Our request to see our families was refused. Our hearts were heavy going back into the van to be returned to prison to continue our life sentence.

Back in Wormwood Scrubs, the inmates didn't know what to say. "Disgusting, man," Winston Silcott said to me. People all over the Scrubs were upset for us, but what could they say? They poured scorn on the judges, calling them all the names under the sun.

No time was wasted in returning us to our respective prisons. "Power and McIlkenny to the wings. The rest to the vans." I heard Paddy whisper to Gerry, "You must be going to Gartree with me." As ever, we were not told which prisons we were being returned to, but I had a good idea it was going to be Long Lartin for me and John.

Back in the category A vans the handcuffs went on again for the long journey to Worcestershire, stuck inside cages within the vans. The break for grub would be at a police station en route, and the cuffs would remain on throughout, even when we went to the toilet.

It was dark when John and I arrived at Long Lartin. The assistant governor was as cold and indifferent as ever. He sarcastically offered John his "old job back" on the wing. When you're really down you can always depend on some prison official to put the knife in. I disliked this particular AG intensely. He was the last person I wanted to meet, and seeing him now on my first day back reminded me starkly of everything I hated about prisons.

I met my mate Mickey Turner; he just shook his head and said repeatedly, "I'm very, very sorry, Hughie." Others came over, shaking hands and commiserating. Considering that these men were the outcasts of society, many of them showed great compassion. I was grateful and touched by their concern. Others, of course, didn't or couldn't talk about it.

Over the next few days I occupied my time reading the reports of our case in the papers. The *Daily Express* and the *Sun*, predictably, were content to delude themselves and their readers with the notion that "justice has been done. The judges' word should be the end. Close the books. The six are guilty and that's the end of it. A waste of taxpayers' money." You never really come to terms with this kind of coverage, even though you expect nothing more from those papers. Chris Mullin was described as the "loony" MP who backed the "bomb gang." The *Times*, on the other hand, published an article entitled "Three unwise judges" by Robert Kee, the eminent journalist and historian who over the years had publicised the case of the Maguire Seven. He suggested that the worrying thing about the verdict was that "few people expected anything else" from the judges. He reaffirmed our own opinion that from the first few days of the hearing the judges were out to protect the British legal system, whatever the consequences for six innocent people. We were nobodies, penniless Irish immigrants whose lives could easily be dismissed to protect the reputation of the British judicial establishment, a far more worthy cause.

During the week some television programme was reviewing the week's news, which was mainly about our case. Paddy McIlkenny, Dick's brother, came on as strong as ever, and promised on behalf of us all that he wouldn't take this lying down. He drew attention to the support and concern that was coming from all over the world. This case, he said, "will never die. Six innocent men will not rot in prison at the behest of judges who don't want to accept the truth." Peter Barry TD condemned British justice with the use of politically diplomatic language but nevertheless got his point across. The Irish Government, through the Minister for Foreign Affairs, Gerry Collins, expressed dismay. Cardinal Tomás Ó Fiaich said he thought the nationalist community in the North were given little reason to trust in British justice after this verdict. And he was damn right.

All the Irish papers had much the same reaction; but the most revealing point was that few papers, even those sympathetic to the judges, expected any other verdict. It was obvious to the world that the judges were biased against us, so much so that really we never stood a chance.

We had many letters from people expressing their sadness at the decision; all of them had the same message: "You'll be back." Some people who wrote had been writing to me for years, and were almost part of my life. Kathleen Doody wrote almost every two weeks, and if I had responded it would have been more frequent: I always owed her a letter. Each of us had a few faithful people who took it on themselves to write to us shortly after our conviction and never stopped writing.

Eileen came to visit me after the judgement, and the visit was anything but cheerful. However, it wasn't sad either: we were both a lot wiser. I could be more honest with Eileen now, not having to put a brave face on things and give her reassurances that everything would be all right when I knew it wasn't. This time Eileen knew from the papers and from having attended the court herself that all was not well; but she spoke, as I did, of the "next time." The hardest part of a visit is walking away at the end; but at the same time I was glad to get the visit over with. Continuously hiding your true feelings and emotions from people close to you is very hard.

Soon after the verdict, Lord Denning, the former Lord Chief Justice, appeared on a television programme that was examining miscarriages of justice. He suggested that public confidence in the law was more important than "one or two" innocent people being convicted wrongly. He criticised Chris Mullin for doing a "great disservice" to British justice, and commented that the writer of the *Times* editorial would have been up for contempt of court in the old days! He was expressing openly what most judges no doubt felt privately. The unpalatable truth was that there was hardly a judge in England who would be prepared to exonerate us without sustained international pressure and, if it were possible, even more new evidence.

I was given a copy of the news magazine *Magill* to read in October 1988. It contained one of the best articles ever written about our plight, by Bishop Edward Daly. He wrote: "I was alarmed and disturbed ... by the attitude of the judges and the nature and tone of their interventions on occasions. To my mind they displayed a considerable degree of bias against the appellants. They also displayed an inability to grasp the difficulties and behaviour of poor people who are unemployed. There was an unbridgeable cultural gap between the judges and the appellants." On his return to hear the verdict in January 1988, Bishop Daly witnessed an extraordinary event at the Old Bailey, when Peter Barry was thoroughly searched. "I could not imagine a former British Foreign Secretary being subjected to the same treatment if he were attending court in Dublin. I could imagine the outcry. After the verdict, heading for Belfast, I thought of the people in graves in Derry and the six men in prison in England. I thought of all the obscene violence and injustices in our society and of the victims of those two evils. And I wept."

I gradually settled back to life in Long Lartin. They gave me a cleaning job, which finished early. In the morning Cyril Birkett, a tough Yorkshireman who would talk endlessly and was great company, used to go through all the papers with me. We would read every paper from cover to cover. Then we would pick out the horses at various race meetings, make our morning snack, and while away the time talking and swapping opinions on the horses running that day.

When I met Geraldine's future husband, Arthur, on a prison visit I liked him instantly. He was a friendly Birmingham lad whose family came from Derry. We talked easily and shared the same interest in football. Above all I was pleased that Geraldine had met someone who would make her happy. When she married, in 1988, she came in to see me a few days afterwards on her own. She was full of her wedding and how well it had gone. Later the piece of wedding cake she left for me created problems for the screws, who chose, with some unexplainable spite, to refuse to give it to me. I didn't waste time arguing or pleading with them; Joe Whitty arranged for me to receive the piece of wedding cake without further fuss.

The campaigns were huge now, and our mail was getting bigger and bigger. Almost monthly we were being sent money by Bob Dawson, raised by members of the London campaign through public meetings and socials. We received information about the activities in Birmingham, London, Sheffield, Nottingham, Stockport, Derby, Oxford, Southampton, Milton Keynes, Manchester, Glasgow, and Dublin. Somehow the efforts of those working in Birmingham were special, because they took risks facing a still largely hostile or at best indifferent public. Eileen herself went out—anonymously—on the Birmingham streets getting signatures for a petition to the Home Secretary. People were polite in the main, but sometimes she received abuse about "those IRA bastards"; others wished that we would "rot in prison." That used to upset her, but she would be back out the next weekend doing the same thing. I thought she was very brave. I always used to say to her, "It's hard in here, but I couldn't do what you do." There were some letters to treasure, especially those from children. A national school teacher from the Boys' School, Castlecomer, County Kilkenny, allowed her pupils to write to me. The letters were so charming and innocent I have still got them today. Stephen Walsh, aged seven, wrote: "It looks like our prayers will be answered. I congratulate you. Me and the class are having a party when you come out. Please come and visit us. I knew you were innocent all along. I hope you will come out in time for our party. A bag of love from Stephen Walsh." Another from the same class simply said, "We are all delighted you will be home soon and the war will be over. I knew you were innocent. Love David Comerford." Kevin Ryan wrote, "Dear Hugh, I am seven years old. My best friend is Damien Carroll. I know you are innocent. I hope you will come to the boys' school. I hope you will soon enjoy your freedom. Love from your friend Kevin Ryan." I received similar letters from schoolchildren everywhere in Ireland. Receiving letters from children was something special and left you with a good feeling that the world out there wasn't so bad after all.

For almost a year we had been reading about the West Midlands Serious Crimes Squad. There were several revelations concerning individual policemen, with complaints coming in all the time from people who felt they had been wrongly treated by the West Midlands police. In July 1989 the squad was disbanded. We found out that even during our appeal one of the detectives who interviewed me was already under investigation for serious misconduct. Another of my interrogators was moved from his work and given a desk job. Nothing serious ever happened to any of them. Another one involved in our interrogation retired from the police and became a Tory mayor in Staffordshire.

We were frustrated and at times angry at the lack of courage of the Irish Government. When the pressure was piled on after the 1987 appeal they were finally shamed into action; but never, even after the release of the Guildford Four, did a single Government minister come right out and say these men were innocent. They spoke of our "possible innocence" and of a "possible miscarriage of justice"—it was disgraceful and cowardly. David Andrews, Niall Andrews, Peter Barry and other individual TDs were excellent and put pressure in Government circles where it was needed, but we were in no doubt that these good people were not at liberty to speak on behalf of the Irish Government.

My recollections of this period in our struggle are not retold with bitterness. It is simply the truth.

English MPs like Tony Benn, Chris Mullin and Jeremy Corbyn were much more straightforward in their belief in our innocence than most of their counterparts in Ireland. Chris Mullin was working away in Parliament and outside; a motion signed by 175 MPs from all parties called for an independent enquiry. The Dublin support committee organised several public meetings at which British MPs, including Tony Benn and Chris Mullin, spoke. Gareth also spoke in Dublin. Tony Benn wrote me a beautiful letter after the appeal, full of concern and expressing his hope that we would win through in the end. He was totally convinced of our innocence, and said so on a television programme without any qualifications. He also gave me a book, *Arguments for Socialism*, signed with a lovely message inside. Another English MP, Joan Maynard, was in close contact with some of the wives for years, and they regarded her as a person who did her best for them with little power on her side. A leading figure in the Liverpool Irish community called Tommy

Walsh was very active and vocal on our case. He wrote endlessly to us. At a meeting arranged in the House of Commons committee rooms he reminded his audience that he could have been speaking about six corpses if the death penalty was still on the statutes.

In December 1989 a big event took place in Dublin on our behalf. I couldn't believe my eyes when I saw it on a video. It was called the "Parade of Innocence." Ten thousand people marched through Dublin, led by Paul Hill and Gerry Conlon. At the front of the march, in pride of place, were all our relatives, including my brothers Charlie and Noel, holding a banner saying *Free the Birmingham Six*. It was the first time I got a sense of the scale of the support for us in Ireland. It almost made me weep to see the thousands and thousands of people on the march, calling for our freedom in the capital city of Ireland. Other prisoners heard about it and they wanted to see the video too. A French prisoner sitting next to me got really excited about it, and later, while we were both getting hot water in our flasks before bang-up for the night, he amused me by singing "Innocent," adding my name to the title.

From late 1988 onwards I would say it was difficult for all of us to be just ordinary prisoners. The media—which had helped put us behind bars—were daily clamouring for our story, for new angles to cover, for statements and direct quotes from us. But we were all much wiser and had become skilled in being selective about what to say to them and how much information to give them.

I kept my head cool, and did as much as possible of the ordinary everyday things that all the inmates engaged in. I continued to exercise every day, rain or shine. I didn't play football any more, but I became a good hand at fixing football boots. I remembered my father doing the same, and I used to say to fellows who asked where I learnt to do it that I must have picked it up from my father, who could do anything with his hands. I also used to do blokes' haircuts. I started by doing a young lad who was having a special visit. He was pleased and he told others, and in the end I had regular customers.

I liked watching films, but not the television: there were always arguments in the television room over which channel should be on. I hated arguments, and always walked away. I had a reputation for being a kind of film buff. I knew all the actors, even in B films; I was always asked my opinion of films, especially those from before the seventies.

Anything that helped you get by in prison had to be used. I observed some inmates over the years who had no interests in anything or anybody. They would sit for hours in their cells, not mixing; no books, no radio, no exercise—just staring into space. It must have been extremely hard for such prisoners to cope in prison; time must have passed so slowly.

Cyril Birkett and I shared a lot of laughs. We had similar tastes. I didn't mix an awful lot with John or Gerry: we each had our own circle of friends, though we often chatted about the case, especially if there was something new coming up. We met also when our legal people visited. But over the years I was never particularly close friends with any of them, though I enjoyed their company when we met. Some guys seemed always to end up in the same prison as me—Paddy, for example—but another guy, called Ray Peck, a good mate, followed me everywhere. He was great fun, always involved in whatever was going on. If there was any trouble in the prison, he was there. He hated the screws, and loved to see them challenged. Ray and I had some good laughs over the years, and he was always on my side and used to be really disappointed when we got knock-backs.

The inmates I befriended varied a great deal in character, but I liked ordinary people who enjoyed the simple pleasures of life. I wasn't interested in politics, and tended to stay away from arguments about the "state of the nation" and the like. I preferred a good chat about football, the films, or songs. Eileen brought me in records from time to time, which I enjoyed listening to when I didn't have the radio on. Despite all the fuss and all the famous people who came to see us, I was always more comfortable and at home with ordinary working-class people.

During 1988 and 1989, Gareth continued to dig for new evidence. She travelled the length and breadth of the country speaking to people who could give any information, however small or insignificant it might have appeared to them. Gareth left no stone unturned. By the end of December 1989 she was able to compile a dossier of new evidence, which was presented to the Home Office. Chris Mullin continued to raise our case in the House of Commons at every opportunity.

Many witnesses—both police officers and civilians—were now prepared to come forward to speak the truth. Among these was a Lancashire policeman who had been on court security duty at Lancaster during our 1975 trial. While West Midlands police were waiting to give evidence against us at the "trial within a trial", he heard them boasting how they had terrorised us. Those same officers then went into court and swore on oath that they had done nothing of the kind.

Another witness was a neighbour of a police officer who was in Morecambe police station when the other five men were interrogated. The officer told his neighbour he was aware they had been physically abused. Two other people living in Morecambe stated that different Lancashire officers had told them much the same story: that the five men were ill-treated and brutalised at Morecambe police station.

A man who was a publican in Birmingham and who had known some of us said he was pressured by the police who came into the pub into changing his evidence.

A chilling account was given by a barman who worked in a pub in Kingstanding. He said that petrol bomb attacks on Irish clubs and homes that occurred in the wake of the pub bombings were organised from his pub, with the knowledge of the police. He had actually said so in a statement taken by police at the time, but this had never previously come out.

Another piece of telling evidence was from a man who worked in the Induction Section at Winson Green Prison. He was the first civilian to see us when we arrived at the prison. Most importantly, he had seen us when we came through reception and *before* we were beaten up by prison officers in the showers. This man's job was to pass us our prison clothes. As we undressed, he saw marks and injuries all over our bodies that were one or two days old.

A police officer who had been on duty at Queen's Road police station revealed that he had told the Devon and Cornwall inquiry how he was ordered not to keep custody records on the night of 22 November 1974.

Other officers gave evidence on the crucial question of the times at which the five at Morecambe were interviewed by the West Midlands officers. The police at our trial persistently maintained, under oath, that no interviews took place with West Midlands officers—and indeed that they had not been allowed access to the men—until after 9.30 a.m. on 22 November. Now officers were coming forward with clear evidence that West Midlands police had been with the five from at least 7.00 a.m.

By October 1989, Gareth was convinced that she had enough new evidence to go back to the Home Secretary to have the case reopened again. The growing awareness that we were suffering a grave injustice was gathering its own momentum. Among those people who knew what had happened to us but who had kept quiet for years, there emerged a spontaneous expression of guilt, concern, and a feeling that they could no longer stay silent. It was a significant breakthrough.

In October 1989 Gareth rang the prison and I was allowed to take the call. "I've got some very good news for you. I'm getting new evidence together. This time we're going to win." To hear Gareth talking like this was unbelievable—she was always so cautious. "That's terrific news, Gareth," I said. A principal officer was listening. I said it slowly and deliberately again. She told me to pass on the news to John and Gerry, and that she would be in to visit us shortly. "I'll break the hundred-yards sprint record to tell them." The PO couldn't wait to get his spoke in. "That must be damn good news, Callaghan." "Yes, it is. You'll hear about it soon," and I left him guessing. I went down immediately to get a visiting order. The PO.who witnessed my receiving the call said he understood what my good news was about. I rang Eileen and told her to tell Geraldine.

Gareth called to see Gerry, John and myself shortly afterwards. She told us the new evidence was very good. She would be submitting it immediately to the Home Office. She was very pleased and very optimistic. This new material was very important. However, she was concerned to protect the privacy of the people who came forward. She asked us not to breathe a word of it to the media or anyone else. She wanted the Home Office to have a chance to respond. Excited though we were, we kept quiet. The press had an inkling but we just said, "no comment."

A new submission to the Home Office went in from Gareth on 18 December 1989. She didn't want the Home Office only to examine the new evidence but additionally to look again at how our case had been handled from the beginning: the widespread use of violence, the fact that there were no safeguards, how we were deprived of food and sleep and threatened for long periods and the mass of complete contradictions in police accounts of the times and manner in which interviews were supposed to have taken place.

The Home Office responded in March 1990 by asking Devon and Cornwall police to re-investigate. They were to consider the treatment we received in police stations, investigate our claims of violence and intimidation, the reason for the lack of custody records, and the quality of the interviews carried out by the police.

A month later, in January, the news broke, and we were besieged with calls, letters and visits from the press for our reaction. From that moment on the press never rested. We were big news.

The other prisoners were surprised when I got a phone call one evening just before bang-up time; we were rarely let take a call at that time. It was a newspaper reporter, asking me how I felt. Was this going to be the last time? I was a lot wiser than him, I thought, and I wouldn't comment. Gareth wouldn't like us being too optimistic about our good news. The BBC rang, and I noticed that now we were the Birmingham Six, not the "pub bombers." Other calls followed.

The assistant governor had me in his office next morning. "Look, Callaghan, I'd appreciate it if you didn't talk to the press or television." "Well," I said, "considering the circumstances, how would you feel?" But I realised if it had been anywhere else I would have been nicked. Talking live to television or radio was strictly against the rules. I just walked away; that morning I didn't give a damn.

The fact was that Gareth had high hopes of succeeding this time, and that was good enough for me. No doubt Paddy, Billy and Dick would be reading and reading the new information: they could chew over complex evidence for breakfast and comprehend it easily. I was happy to wait and see.

In the meantime another momentous event happened to all of us. I was called at an unusual time, just before bang-up for the night, to be told by the assistant governor that our status as category A prisoners had been changed to category B. Never, as far as we knew, had this happened to so-called IRA prisoners before, nor indeed to men who were doing life for similar crimes. Your status might change just before you were due to be released, but not any other time. This was completely unexpected. Overnight we were no longer to be regarded as "highly dangerous men, likely to be a threat to society." The immediate reality for us was that we could now have anyone visit us.

I couldn't believe it. Then a flood of words came pouring out. "It just shows you what we have been saying all along. They know about us. They know we're innocent people." I laughed and said to the governor, "I would've lost a good few bob if I'd bet any of the five that we'd never come off the book." I always believed they would never take us off, to maintain the public's belief that we were guilty. "They fitted us up, but this proves another point, guv: they must be under a lot of pressure if they were forced to take us off. If they really believed we were IRA men they would never, ever have removed us off the book." Of course we will never really know how long ago it was that they ceased believing we were guilty. Our changing status now was just a public admission of a view I believe they had held privately for a long time.

I felt totally victorious as I stood up to leave the AG's office. He reminded me rather feebly that it was yet to be confirmed, but I knew it was real.

I ran into my mate Cyril; he was the first one in prison I wanted to tell. "I've backed a few winners in my time with you, but I never would have won this bet. I've just been told I'm off the book. All six of us, we're all off the book." Cyril was amazed. "You're not guilty. That's what that means." Now, as John Walker said to me, we could sleep at night. For fifteen years we were checked throughout the night, and now they won't come near us. It was an extraordinary feeling of release, as if a permanent dark shadow that hung around at night had suddenly vanished.

When the news was confirmed I went straight to the AG's office to get visiting orders for people I always wanted to visit me but who would have had to be investigated first, which I wouldn't put people through. The AG was full of comment, almost suggesting I should be grateful. "Listen," I said, "it's still more important for me to prove my innocence, whatever status I have, than coming off the book. I shouldn't be here in the first place."

One more significant feature of category B visits was the removal of the dogs. What a relief that was for me! I never got completely over the fear of these animals, though it declined a bit over the years. Screws were reasonable about it in the end, and my escorts would keep the dogs at a distance; nevertheless I was always and ever alert when I saw the dogs appearing.

One of the first visitors I had under the new status was Sister Sarah. I thanked her for all her letters and all the money she sent in over the years. I was delighted to be able at last to thank her in person.

Another person who came to visit was Ludovic Kennedy. I was really excited and a little nervous about meeting him. I remembered how I felt when I read his article in the *Sunday Times* about us. "I accuse," he titled it, and it was a very strong condemnation of the judges. "These six men should not be in prison. The British legal system is keeping them there, having corrupted the police and the judiciary into incarcerating them against common justice ..." I had read the article with immense pleasure and gratitude, and it was great now to be able to thank the man in person.

I recognised him as soon as we walked in. He stood up, and John and I gave him a warm welcome. He referred to a piece I had written in the *Independent* about food we could take back from visits. It was limited to cartons of juice and fresh bananas. I wrote that I liked bananas because they made a nice sandwich for supper time. "I read your article in the paper and I tried to get you some fresh bananas on the way up the motorway, but I couldn't get them till we reached Evesham. But they wouldn't let me take them in to you after all." He bought me sweets and drinks at the tuck shop to make up for it.

We talked a good deal. He knew our case intimately and talked freely about it. He was very reassuring, and expressed his confidence that we would be going back to the Court of Appeal. He was much more optimistic than John or me, I have to confess. He told us all about the Cooper and MacMahon case and about his discussions with Lord Lane. I understood the significance of what he was talking about, and I knew he helped get those people off that conviction.

When Geraldine's baby was born, I was delighted to have become a grandfather. She was just a few weeks old when Geraldine brought her in to see me; I held her for the whole two hours. It was a beautiful feeling. Birmingham women visiting their husbands or sons came over to me, admiring the new baby as only mothers can and wishing us well, expressing the hope that I would soon be outside, able to enjoy the company of my grandchild. "It's not right you being in here," a woman with a Birmingham accent said to me. "Your day will come soon, you'll see."

In October 1989 the Guildford Four—Gerry Conlon, Paul Hill, Carol Richardson, and Paddy Armstrong—were suddenly released. It came on the news one night, and the next day they were out. It was just incredible, and it set my adrenalin flowing. That night the television room was packed. Prisoners were standing on chairs and tables, and huge cheers went up when we saw them. Gerry Conlon was in Long Lartin, and many of the prisoners knew him; he had some good mates here. When he rushed over to the cameras and made that speech ending with "The Birmingham Six are innocent. The Maguires are innocent ..." a surge of emotion ran through me. Good for you, Gerry!

We were elated by his release. Ours would soon follow. There was a great sense of victory among the prison population that night.

Charlie Haughey made a statement a month later in the

Dáil. It was a good speech but, if I might say so, a little late. Nevertheless it was the best yet from any Taoiseach since we were convicted. "The release of the Guildford Four brought widespread feelings of relief throughout this country. At the same time the revelations that such serious miscarriages of justice can occur has caused equally widespread feelings of unease and dismay. It has major implications for the case of the Birmingham Six. I believe that the arguments for reopening the case of the Birmingham Six are now so persuasive that they are impossible to withstand."

The impact of the release of the Guildford Four created an onslaught of demands to the Home Secretary to take action now to avoid another tragedy; but the wall of silence round the Home Office stayed. Even Denning was persuaded to make the comment that "in a sense, after the Guildford Four and particularly with the suggestions against the West Midlands police there is certainly a case for reconsideration ... It does give room for disquiet. But on the other hand it is a very difficult decision whether it should be reopened or not." He was later to change his mind again—the prerogative of an old man who seemed not to share the human feelings of small mortals like the six of us.

Shortly after he was released, Gerry Conlon came to visit us. The screws couldn't cope; their faces said it all. Gerry was popular with the prisoners, but the screws couldn't stand him, or Paul Hill. They were strong, defiant, young, and innocent. The screws rarely got the better of them in prison. Now here was Gerry sitting in the visiting room, a free man. He vowed to fight for us, to speak wherever he could, and of course he was certain about our imminent release and exoneration. Prisoners asked if they could get to see Gerry. One did, and forfeited a visiting order to see him. Paul Hill came to visit us on two occasions. He brought with him on one of those visits Courtney Kennedy, the niece of the late Jack Kennedy and daughter of Robert Kennedy. She was a delightful American woman, very friendly and charming. John and I had an easy rapport with her. I recalled to her my lasting memory of where I was the night her Uncle Jack died. Paul was quiet, looked well, and still had the long lanky hair and lean look. The screws looked as sick as parrots seeing these lads walking in with the famous Kennedy. As they were leaving, John said to Courtney, "Give my regards to Broadway," and I said, "That's a cue for a song, John," and there in the visiting rooms right up close to the screws' table we started to sing.

A screw back on the wing later remarked, "I see you have been entertaining the Kennedys." "That's how it goes," I said and walked away, laughing to myself. Joe Kennedy made a flying visit to us also, again accompanied by Paul. He was an impressive young man who told us of his efforts in America on our behalf. He had some difficulty getting into England, though his visit to us was widely broadcast and of great political significance for our case abroad, especially in America.

I had a succession of visitors, from journalists to campaign people. When famous people came in it was difficult sometimes to know what to say to them. Their faces and their voices were familiar, yet they were strangers. Sometimes it was a strain; at least I found it so. I used to observe Paddy on visits when we were in Gartree together, and he seemed to experience no such strain. It was the other way round: the visitors found it hard to say anything because Paddy always had so much to say.

It was terrific nevertheless to have so many people interested in me wanting to visit me as well. Most visits were very pleasant.

Often, however, after the strain of talking endlessly about the only thing we had in common, "the case of the Birmingham Six," I would go back to the room mentally and physically exhausted, though always in good form.

Peter Barry came every time he was in England. I always liked him. Many of the TDs were treated indifferently by the prison authorities: they were stuck out in the public visiting room, despite their status as members of the Dáil. I complained and said it wasn't right, that their British counterparts didn't receive this kind of treatment. They immediately assumed that I was looking for special privileges. "Not always possible to get rooms," they said; but arrangements gradually improved, and when it was possible they gave us a private room.

When I met Jeremy Corbyn I thought he was terrific. He was a slightly built man, with strong opinions, whole-heartedly on the side of the working folk and with no time at all for any part of the British establishment; he thought the judges were very biased against ordinary people. He was a good friend of Chris Mullin. I knew the two of them got some stick from the gutter papers, and when you met people like him you couldn't but admire them for their concern and courage. We had a visit from a group of people from Newark who were campaigners. There were about eight or nine of them. It was a lovely cheerful, easy visit. Drink flowed freely, from lemonade bottles, though its effects were quite strong. Later, back in John's cell, a screw remarked: "This place smells like a brewery." We offered no comment. It was a memorable visit, full of laughter and optimism.

Among those who came to see us were people from the Irish Commission for Prisoners Overseas. Nuala Kelly, from Enniskillen, used to come to the prison to visit all kinds of Irish prisoners, not just us. She was always very forthright, and the screws weren't too keen. Nuala was a very pleasant, committed person who knew all there was to know about Irish prisoners' rights. The ICPO visited our families in Belfast and other parts of Ireland. I wished that such organisations had existed earlier: we could have done with their shoulders to lean on, and so could our wives and children. Nuala was at the appeal also, along with Monsignor Hannon, who headed the ICPO in Dublin.

David Andrews was a regular visitor. He was a friendly man, easy to talk to, and asked lots of questions. He had a terrific sense of humour. He knew I liked a little bet on the horses, and he used to put bets on for me and ring the solicitor's office if I won! He also got a friend of his to send me a fabulous book about horses and the art of betting. On one visit I could sense he wanted to talk officially. He brought up the subject of parole. "Would you not consider parole, and fight for your innocence on the outside? You've been long enough in here." I was emphatic. No, we didn't want parole. "Are you sure you wouldn't consider it? The Government and our people at the embassy can talk to the Home Secretary about it." No, no parole, and no pardons. He meant well, but he had no idea of the significance for us of accepting parole. To be even considered for parole you had to show by your attitude and behaviour that you were full of remorse for the crimes you had committed, and demonstrate a willingness to make amends. It was unthinkable, I told him, even if we had to spend the rest of our days in prison. The only people who should be showing remorse were the police, who lied and continued to lie. The question of parole continued to be raised, but not again by David Andrews.

Sir John Farr, who declared his belief in our innocence and his disappointment at the judgement, appealed to the Home

Secretary for mercy. But that wasn't what we wanted either, however kind and well-meaning he was. We were coming out with our names cleared. I had resolved that if they ever forced parole or a pardon on me they would have to carry me out. I knew this to be the case for all of us. The pressure on the judiciary was immense; the scandal of the judges' behaviour at the last appeal continued to be raised. Dumping us out with parole might have been an easy option for them now, but we would never accept it.

I wrote to Heather Mills, the court correspondent of the *Independent*, when we came off the book. She replied and said she would like to come and visit me. She didn't declare her credentials: she put herself down as a friend. She had some guts; if she had been found out they wouldn't let her in again. I urged her to be careful. She ran a little story, and then came to see me again on a visit. Many more followed. I found her easy to talk to, and she had a very good understanding of our case. Another story appeared; and this time the assistant governor called me in and read the riot act. "Let me make it quite clear to you. I read that article. She is a journalist, and will only be permitted to see you again as a friend." Every day hundreds of people were writing about us in every kind of publication, and here he was telling me that Heather was breaking the rules. They're rattled, I thought; they can't stand the pressure now; and I was pleased to see it, even at this small level.

I wrote regularly to the letters page of the *Irish News*. Once I wrote to Tom Samways, who had been a journalist for years in London, and told him how fond I was of his nostalgic columns in the *Irish News*, and how I once sold the paper as a youngster from Flax Street. I said I hoped to meet him in Flax Street some day and tell him a story of my own. He wrote back a beautiful letter, telling me it would be a pleasure to meet me in Flax Street. He published my letter in the form of a story; but we never were to meet, as he died shortly afterwards.

A journalist from the *Irish News* came to visit me, Séamus Kelters. He was full of news about home and the various reactions and speculation about our case. Then he sprang a surprise on me. The editor of the *Irish News* had conveyed his good wishes, and invited me to write a weekly column for the paper.

"Me? You're joking!"

"No, I'm serious."

"You mean write about the case?"

"No, anything you care to write about."

"About my life and times in Belfast maybe?"

"If you like."

I told him that everything went through the censors. But it didn't stop my letters getting through, he pointed out, and they'd had a terrific response to them. "Anyway, think about it," he said.

"No, I don't need to. I'll do it."

We shook hands on the deal. I went back to my cell and thought of all the things I'd like to write about—I particularly wanted to write about my old days. Séamus published an excellent article about the visit in the *Irish News* a week later. He wrote eloquently and with great understanding of my situation.

I started to write regularly, and I used to occupy my mind walking round the yard thinking about what I would say in that column. The paper decided to call it "Jail Journal." I sent the first article to Séamus, and he wrote back, "Great stuff. Your column will be in this Friday, and every Friday after that." I couldn't wait to see it. When it came out the first article was entitled "An innocent lifer's form of escapism." In it I described how I escaped from the reality of my surroundings when out in the exercise yard. Patsy sent me in the paper with a lovely letter, proud and delighted that I could do this. It was a funny feeling reading my own name on an article in the paper I had read since I was a nipper and had stood on street corners selling it.

I wrote about fourteen articles for the *Irish News*, and it was a great pastime. I used to sit till two o'clock some mornings writing them; I would write pages and pages, then rip the whole lot up and start again. Gradually I got the hang of it, and sometimes I would have two pieces ready to go at the same time. In the main they were about my days in Belfast or my early years in Birmingham. They put funny titles on them though: "Crumlin Road Bogart and the decline of the flicks"; "A walk down the Pad"—the Pad being Butler Street, where I was born and reared. "Losing a day's pay for a classic" described my day at the great England-Ireland match in 1947 in Liverpool. They were simple articles; I visualised ordinary people in all parts of Belfast identifying with them.

I had to be in the mood to write, and often to help set the mood I used to put on John Bennett's "Sunday Club" programme. In no time my mind would be miles away from my prison cell; I was back home in Belfast. Just writing the articles was a therapy and a form of escape. I had a terrific response from people at home. My old friend Paddy Cassidy wrote; he was delighted for me and reminded me of old times together and how far apart and how different our paths were now.

Eileen came in on a visit with an article written by Peter Rhodes of a Wolverhampton paper, the *Express and Star*. It was an insulting article, condemning us for getting all this attention; we were convicted of murder and were being treated like celebrities. Eileen wanted me to write back to him, but I disagreed and said I couldn't be bothered responding to every lousy article, otherwise my time would be spent in the negative pursuit of people who didn't want to read or write about facts staring them in the face. However, I got my opportunity some time later, and very unexpectedly. Gerry Hunt came on a visit with a journalist in tow. I asked him if he knew Peter Rhodes, and later on in the visit when we had been talking for some time I said I wouldn't mind meeting him.

A few days later Peter Rhodes came to visit. I was all keyed up, and wondered after all what I would say to him face to face. Eileen rang a few days later and was laughing. "I don't know what you said to him. He's changed his tune completely." In fact I had said very little, just spoke to him about the case, our interrogation by the West Midlands police, the fear we went through, and our years in prison as innocent people. "If this guy is an IRA man, I will eat my hat," Peter Rhodes wrote in an article a few days later.

"Prison forums" were held regularly on every topic under the sun. It was believed to be good for prisoners to bare their souls in little groups, sharing their thoughts with other prisoners, screws, and the probation and welfare people. Sometimes doctors, psychologists or outside specialists would attend. I rarely attended them; I wasn't able or willing to share my private feelings in this way, especially with screws all around. Let them know your vulnerable areas and they would exploit them in your low moments. But some prisoners benefited from them. The other reason I didn't attend was the fact that we could never bring up the subject of our case, though it would have been very helpful in the early days to talk to somebody about it. Now there was no longer the desperate desire to talk. A long time later John and I were unexpectedly given an opportunity to be filmed on television walking around the exercise yard following a prison forum meeting.

The opportunity to reiterate our determination not to accept parole was taken by us when the BBC were invited to the prison to film a prison forum meeting. John and I took part in these discussions. The BBC approached us and asked us if they could get clearance from Joe Whitty to film us, would we agree? We laughed and agreed, not expecting the governor to entertain the idea. But he did.

John and I walked around the exercise yard, followed by the television crews. Later on in an interview we unequivocally stated that we would not consider parole, and restated our determination to walk out of prison as innocent men cleared of any involvement in the Birmingham bombings. The BBC showed us in our prison overcoats. It was the first time we had been seen on television. Every time our pictures appeared in the papers they used the ones taken at the time of our arrest. Comments were made later about how different we looked. There was no doubt about that; John and I were sixteen years older. The little hair we had left was very grey indeed. Radio Four ran the story, "Birmingham Six men refuse to consider parole." A recording of the interview was broadcast in full. I saw this coverage as being of great significance to us. It was a very good opportunity to speak for ourselves on the question of parole which was currently being debated and written about at great length by the media. After the programme the AG spoke to me and remarked about his own belief that I meant what I said. He told me he had said to his wife, "Callaghan is a man of his word. He would have to be carried out."

In the meantime, by March 1990, the chief constable of the West Midlands police was asked by the Home Office to provide a report on the activities of his police. He referred the matter to the Devon and Cornwall police, and asked them to investigate the West Midlands police.

The stream of people coming to visit never let up as the case for a return to the Court of Appeal became more and more inevitable. It included MPs from both sides, TDs, American congressmen, members of various European parliaments, and journalists writing for practically every English newspaper at some time or another. Paul Foot was a very witty man with an upper-class English accent; he could take the judiciary apart. We had a terrific conversation with him about the Carl Bridgewater case, which he wrote a book about. The head of the Irish Chaplaincy came, Father Bobby Gilmore, a cool Galway man who, despite the disquiet of senior church officials in the Westminster Diocese, had agreed to be the chairman of the National Birmingham Six Campaign when it wasn't popular to be a supporter or associated with us.

Our afternoons now were taken up with visits. Some days we didn't stop for a minute. It was certainly stimulating, though none of us were under any illusions; many of our visitors just came to have a look.

I was constantly receiving requests to leave visiting orders at the gate. Gerry got fed up of it in the end, and seldom came towards the end of our time in Long Lartin. I would always remember the treatment we had for years after 1975 from many journalists and newspaper editors. Now they all wanted our story.

Lord Denning could not contain himself and felt compelled

to enter the picture again and comment on all the news coverage concerning our case and the Guilford and Maguire cases. He gave an interview to a right-wing magazine, the *Spectator*. He reflected on all the attention we were all getting, and concluded that if we had been hanged there would have been no fuss about us; we would have been forgotten and the community quite satisfied. I dwelt on this for weeks. After all we had been through, how could anyone, least of all a judge, make such a statement! He was condemned by many for his comments. Paddy McIlkenny said, "The question is, is he expressing his own view or that of the rest of the judges?" Denning knew damn well what he was saying, and it hurt our families to be told it would have been better all round if we had been hanged.

In total frustration one evening, and still brooding over Denning's hateful interview, I went over to the screws' table. I wanted to prove to myself whether these guys were as inhuman and uncaring as they appeared all the time; I wanted to know what they really thought. It was totally out of character for me. I started to question them on what they believed about our case. I asked them if they believed everyone in prison was guilty. Quick as a flash, without pausing for thought, one of them said, "Yes, I do." One said he had read what Denning said and, though he believed we might be innocent, he thought Denning had a point. The system rested its foundations on the British courts and judges. Their attitude was to support the system, right or wrong. If there were victims, that was too bad. "Even if people are innocent?" I asked. "It's not the individual you think about," the screws said. "It's the system we support."

In August 1990 we were called to the governor's office and handed a piece of paper. Gerry read out the contents: our case was going back to the Court of Appeal for the third time. We were beaming with smiles, and hugged each other in delight. We knew without any doubt that this was it. We were on our way out; after fifteen years our struggle was coming to an end.

In August 1990 there was an announcement that new scientific examinations had discovered discrepancies in the notes of an alleged police interview with Dick. The ESDA test, as it was known, used a new electronic device that suggested that the interview notes may not have been written contemporaneously but were written up at separate times on different notepads and using different pens. From that moment on the case had to collapse. The Guildford judge had only recently ruled that if one confession was suspect, then the case against all four fell. Moreover, George Reade, as the officer in charge, had always maintained that he was in full control of the investigations and that interviews were conducted under his direction. The ESDA tests now completely contradicted his and his officers' version of events, in particular the time a specific interview with Dick was said to have taken place. Dick in fact had always maintained that this interview never took place.

In the meantime, unknown to our solicitors, Dr Lloyd, the forensic scientist who had taken swabs of my hands and found me negative, was beavering away quietly in Birmingham and continuing to carry out his own tests. (All the others were swabbed by Skuse.) He had always been dissatisfied with the quality of the scientific tests used to convict Billy, Paddy, Johnny, and Dick. He readily made his work and the results of his experiments available when our case was finally reopened again for the third time. His theory that soap could have been the cause of the positive reaction obtained by Dr Skuse was seized upon and much quoted by the media. (Later Billy Power took a bar of soap in the van with him on the way to the Appeal Court; all the papers the next day had a picture of his hand holding a bar of soap!)

I listened to the last item on the radio news that night. "Just to repeat our main story ..." I had heard it over and over during the evening, but it was still exciting to hear it again just before I nodded off. "The Home Secretary has announced that the case of the Birmingham Six has been referred back to the Court of Appeal for the third successive time. The Home Secretary is doing so in the light of new information discovered by the Devon and Cornwall police."

I lay in my cell that night and thought of all the people who helped bring this about. Gareth Peirce was, of course, the key to it all. She never gave up. Everything after this was a formality: we would go through the motions, but we were going out the gates; of that I was certain. I couldn't sleep, and began to do again what I had done for most of my fifteen years at night: write letters. There were so many people to thank. Where would I begin?

13

VICTORY

So sure was I that I would never be returning to Long Lartin that this time I gave most of my possessions away, in the time-honoured tradition. I gave my little radio, which had seen me through many dark nights since I bought it from an inmate twelve years earlier for a fiver, to a young lad serving life; I hoped it would give him as much pleasure as it gave me over the years. My picture of woods and lakes that I treasured and took to every cell since Albany I had given away some months earlier to a prisoner who used to come into my cell just to look at it.

I was sad to leave some good mates behind. I didn't make any promises about coming back to visit: I would have to wait and see how I would cope with that. I promised Jimmy Robinson that we would use the media to publicise the case of the Bridgewater Four, as Gerry Conlon had done for us.

Reflecting on my time in Long Lartin and the other prisons I was in, I look back on the Probation Service and how probation officers generally treated me. I have very little to thank them for. However, one probation officer was an exception. John Wain, a probation officer in Long Lartin, will be remembered by me as a very decent man, who treated me well and always with respect.

We said goodbye to everyone and made our way to reception for the ride to London.

On the way over, Gerry spotted a security van, used for transporting category A prisoners. Throughout our sixteen years we had been transported in these cages. The reception area was packed with screws, eager, it seems, to accompany us with a top-security escort all the way to London. My blood started to boil. There was no way we were travelling anywhere, not even round the corner, in the A vans. The security people were clearly doing this to show their contempt for us. "Listen," I told them, "we're not going in any A van. What the hell are you playing at?" I was not prepared at the eleventh hour to be treated like this, nor were Gerry or John. I was shouting at the top of my voice. John was telling me to calm down. The screws were very surprised to see me so angry.

The deputy governor was sent for. "Have you a problem? Why don't you get in the van?" "We haven't got a problem, you have!" I demanded my gear back, which had already been placed in the van, and told the deputy governor with a few expletives uncharacteristic of me that they could ring the Home Office. We politely walked away and returned to our cells. If the circumstances had been different I would have been nicked.

I contacted Gareth and explained the situation. She undertook, as usual, to deal with it, and understood without requiring an explanation the significance of our protest.

Back again in my old cell, now stripped bare after my departure, I was still high and giving out like mad about the screws and the deputy. The inmates were delighted at the stand we took, though some of them laughed at the idea that under any circumstances we would have been prepared to spend a minute more in Long Lartin than we needed to! Prisoners, of course, always appreciated blokes who got the better of screws and the system.

We remained another few days in our old cells; then we said our goodbyes again for the umpteenth time. Prisoners were shouting from windows, landings—anywhere they could get a vantage point. "Good luck, lads! Don't come back!" I saw one prisoner smash his window just so he could shout "Good luck!" He obviously thought it was a moment worth getting nicked for. We travelled to London on the eve of the appeal in a comfortable van that we could see out of and move about in. Just looking out at the motorway was a pleasant change after years travelling in cages, hardly able to see out and handcuffed to a screw for the whole journey. In cities we stopped along with all the other traffic at the lights and pedestrian crossings—that was new too. The handcuffs, nevertheless, remained. But our stand on travelling conditions was to be more significant than we realised: Gareth explained to us later that it set the tone for the manner in which we were transported to and from the Court of Appeal in London. We had got the better of stupidity and spite, which epitomised the attitude of so many screws throughout the English prison system.

The atmosphere in the Scrubs was terrific. Billy and Dick gave us a great welcome. We were the main topic of conversation all over the prison. Conditions in the Scrubs had improved considerably since 1987: there were fewer prisoners, cells were spruced up, and there was more room to move about.

On our final visits in the Scrubs we got the red carpet treatment for the first time after sixteen years. Each of us was given a separate cubicle for our visitors. After months of being visited by politicians, churchmen, journalists, and campaigners, this visit was just for our families. It was a beautifully happy event. There were times during the visit when we couldn't believe what was happening. Eileen, Charlie and Patsy were my visitors. We talked about the release; Eileen went over what I would wear in court. We talked about Geraldine and the baby, and Eileen told me about the house they were staying in. It was a visit without strain, without the need for mental effort to please or to reassure. All our big worries would soon be over. We were just days away from release. Life in the outside world would bring a whole lot of new experiences, but for now we were happy. Our fight was won.

There were numerous young women on the visit, the daughters of Dick, Billy, and John. Some of Dick's little grandchildren ran in and out of the cubicle, laughing happily. I heard one of the lads call out, "Where's the champagne?" The women moved freely from cubicle to cubicle, laughing and chatting away to the other men. Eileen remarked that we had come a long way since our visiting days in Albany—"It's a pity they don't treat people like this all the time." How right she was! Patsy looked peaceful and content to let things take their course now. "You'll soon be in Belfast again, when all this is finished." I hadn't seen Charlie for a long time. He could never come to terms with prisons and hardly ever visited, finding it too stressful. But he was in terrific form.

On the eve of the appeal a vigil was organised outside the gates of the Scrubs. We couldn't see out, but the screws told us about it. The gates, they said, were lit up with television lights and the candles held by the crowd. My thoughts turned to Patsy and Charlie, both of whom were taking part in the vigil.

Some papers were saying it would be a day, others a month,

before our release. But there wasn't a single paper, television or radio programme that didn't expect us to win this time; though of course some papers—like the *Sun,* the *Star,* and some regional papers—didn't want to see us released, still preferring to believe that we were guilty and that the great system of British justice couldn't have got it so wrong for so long.

On the ride to the court we were all laughing and joking, though tensions obviously were there too. Going to court any time was an ordeal; but this would be different. We were sure of the outcome, even if we had to sit and listen to the arguments all over again. There were no sirens, no motorcade, just two white vans forming part of the Monday morning traffic in London. As we neared the court Tracy Hunter, Gerry's daughter, and Breda Power ran up to the van and waved in at us. They had time for brief hellos and smiles before we were whisked inside.

Gareth came into the cells with Tony Gifford, Nick Brown, and Ivan Geffen. "Good morning, gentlemen." He went over to Paddy. "Fit and well, Paddy?" "Yes, raring to go." We were escorted up through the building, in the lifts this time. The whole atmosphere and the attitude of the court officials, including the police, had completely changed.

The appeal began on 4 March 1991. The grounds this time were that the confessions had been completely discredited, as a result of an ESDA test that had found discrepancies in Dick's statement. The Director of Public Prosecutions gave notice that the Crown would no longer contend that on the basis of the scientific evidence the convictions were safe and satisfactory. You could be forgiven for thinking that with the collapse of the two main planks of the Crown's case it was all over and we could go home; but the appeal was to last a further ten days. But this time none of us minded. We understood the importance for our barristers of going through the new scientific evidence. There was also new evidence completely discrediting the tests carried out by Dr Skuse.

A retrial would have given us the opportunity to go through the whole case again, but that was denied. We were not to be allowed to go into the beatings, the false confessions, the mental and physical torture, and all the other horrendous events that took place after we were arrested; nor would we be allowed to name again all the policemen we accused in our trial of assault and corruption. Nevertheless the limited opportunity we had was going to be used to demonstrate that what we had been saying all along was true. All of us had repeatedly said that one day the truth would come out; it was this unshakable belief that had kept us going, kept us motivated to keep fighting. We waited sixteen years for the truth to be told, but our day was finally come. Mike Mansfield and Tony Gifford would demonstrate in court once again what they said at the 1987 appeal and what we had all said since 1975: that there *was* a conspiracy, that there *was* mass perjury by policemen, that there *were* mistakes (at the very least) by Dr Skuse.

In the VIP seats sat all our old faithful friends: Chris Mullin, Ludovic Kennedy, Jerry Corbyn, David Andrews, Bishop Edward Daly, Father Bobby Gilmore, Peter Barry, and Sister Sarah Clarke. Also in court were representatives of the Irish embassy in London, most notably Paul Murray, a first secretary, who since his appointment had been very helpful to all our families. He had made several visits to us all in prison. He was a nice man, whom I liked and got on very well with. In the midst of it all, as ever, sat Gareth Peirce, almost hidden by the pile of papers, at the corner of a desk just behind Mike Mansfield and Tony Gifford.

When Mike Mansfield rose he was like a figure from a Shakespeare play. He was in his element; and how I enjoyed watching this drama unfold! Mike set out to expose what he described as the "web of deceit" that overtook the police, some of whom, it could now be clearly proved, had lied in court about important matters of detail concerned with at least one of the confessions. The world knew by now the extent of the lies and perjury, but for the present we had to be content with what could be dealt with at this appeal, even if it resulted in a mere two or three policemen being identified and many other guilty ones escaping the net.

The prosecutor, Graham Boal, had said he could no longer sustain the convictions on the scientific evidence, but proceeded to argue the toss just once more on some of the confessions, which he claimed could still be sustained. We had heard it all before; by now the back pages of the *Sporting Life* would have been more interesting to me than listening to Graham Boal. For eleven days he struggled pathetically to save face for the Crown and to defend the reputation of British justice. At one stage even the judges told him he was merely doing a "damage limitation exercise." Nevertheless there were times when Boal tried to regurgitate old material about some of us being members of the IRA, particularly with reference to John. He dwelt on John's confession for a whole morning; it unnerved John greatly, but we all reassured him. It was hard for many people in the court to understand just what Graham Boal was trying to achieve.

We had a few moans during those eleven days, reminiscent of our earlier times there. The food in the Old Bailey never got any better. We sat for hours in the morning and again in the afternoon in that court having received the barest minimum for our breakfast and lunch. No wonder some of the papers described us as pale and looking a bit lean! My lasting memory of food in prison is that it was both stodgy and insubstantial, and I was always hungry an hour after I ate. Just a few yards away from the entrance to the Old Bailey, we were told, the pub was packed every lunch hour with our people, celebrating already. We couldn't wait to join them. It had proved very difficult for the campaign workers to hire a room or any facilities near the court where our families and the campaigners could spend time together privately away from the glare of the media. It seems the police may have warned proprietors with rooms or office space available near the Court not to rent to anyone connected with the Birmingham Six. When Breda Power and Paul May went to see the City of London chief he claimed that his officers had nothing to do with this. We are expected to believe that places the campaigners had no difficulty in hiring previously were suddenly all booked up. Astonishingly the Police Chief suggested our families and their families and their friends might use premises provided by the police. Paul and Breda declined the invitation.

With just two days to go, Sally Mulready contacted Paul Foot who was then a journalist on the *Daily Mirror*. He worked a miracle. He managed to persuade the newspaper owner, the late Robert Maxwell, to agree to paying for a suite at the exclusive Waldorf Hotel which was just minutes away from the Old Bailey. We were also able to get Maxwell to agree that the Daily Mirror would not make public his very generous offer.

A twenty-page document packed with new evidence was not subsequently used by our defence at the appeal. It included substantial material from interviews the Devon and Cornwall police conducted with police officers who witnessed the events in Morecambe and Queen's Road police stations around the time of our arrest. None of this evidence has even been disclosed to the public.

By the morning of the fourteenth, while Graham Boal was still battling on, Gareth passed us a note saying she didn't think it would be very long now. The judges appeared to have had enough of Mr Boal: it was a case of the longer he spoke the more unconvincing he sounded. He finally concluded his submissions for the Crown and sat down. Tony Gifford rose to make his final speech; it was an emotional moment for all of us. His remarks were memorable and dramatically expressed. The years of suffering and the misery our families endured should end now, he said; "all that remains to be done is to release these men back to society and to their families." With Tony still in the act of sitting down we heard the command we had been given so many times before: "Will the appellants please rise." I thought it was another recess; but this was it, this was the moment we had all waited for. It's the time when your knees do strange things, you feel sweaty and cold at the same time, you can hear your heart pounding. We turned to face the judges. Then the magic words came. As a result of fresh scientific evidence, "the appeal is granted ... you are free to go."

A huge roar came from the gallery. We looked at each other; hugs all round. Everywhere there were scenes of joy and relief. We were waving like children up at the gallery. The women were hugging each other. Gareth came over to us with a beautiful smile on her face; I was as happy for her as I was for myself and the other men. Mike Mansfield said as we shook hands that it was the loudest cheer he had ever heard in court. Ludovic Kennedy was already gone—he was one man I would have liked to thank personally. Bishop Daly was smiling; he had shared in our victory as he had in our sufferings. What could you say to these good people? "Thank you" seemed so feeble: they had saved our lives, rescued us from hell. We would be indebted to them for ever.

We went back to the cells for the last time, to deal with the formalities of discharge and to collect our possessions. Some of us had accumulated a bit more money than others. I had the most: just over a hundred pounds. "You can buy the first round, Callaghan," said Paddy. With police on each side of us we lined up to walk out of the court as free men, exonerated from any connection with the Birmingham pub bombings.

Between Gareth and the campaign people in London, all the arrangements for our departure had been made. Three chauffeur-driven limousines had been hired to take us to a secret location for a private reunion with our families. All the relatives and special friends would follow our cars in two mini-buses. The arrangements were made with great care to ensure that we would be allowed to come out of the front entrance of the Old Bailey with dignity. No tabloid press men or chequebook journalists would be taking us away! We wanted to go out there first and thank the thousands of people who we knew had been with us all along and had queued up since early morning to see us walk out that door. We were hardly listening to the advice of the police about the crowds, the barriers, the press—we just wanted to get out of there. As we lined up to go out the front exit, Paddy, who found himself first in line, came rushing towards the front. "If you think I'm going out last you can think again. I've got something to say. Let me out first." We all laughed and of course gave way to the mighty atom.

We emerged through the front doors to cheers from our families and the crowds. The sun was shining. After years surrounded by high walls, the brightness and colour of everything took me a bit by surprise. We started to applaud the waiting people behind the barriers. Saying "Thank you, thank you" repeatedly, I ran over towards the crowds. We were grabbed and hugged by the people, all expressing joy at our release. In the crowd in front of me I recognised just one face behind the barrier. It was that of a news broadcaster for a local radio station in the midlands, a woman who had supported our case for a long time. Nicola Pullman grabbed me and gave me an emotional hug. "You promised me an interview." "Yes, I know, and I will do it." She produced a microphone. "Say something." "What, now?" "Say something. You are on live." Taken aback, I shouted over the cheers, "Thank you to everyone who helped us. I am very grateful." I moved on, leaving Nicola smiling broadly. I wanted to hug everyone, but all I could do was say "Thank you" from the bottom of my heart as I moved along the barrier. We had not forgotten the faith of ordinary people like ourselves who believed in us.

Six microphones had been placed in front of the assembled press. Each of us in turn said something. We had all thought about what we were going to say, but when the time came, standing there with thousands of people cheering and the cameras of the world facing us, it was impossible to be composed. It still hadn't sunk in that we were free men: I half expected to be escorted away again by a screw.

Billy Power made an important statement shared by us all. He questioned why Judith Ward (who has since been released) and the Bridgewater people remained inside. "They are innocent too." "Every dog has his day," Dick said. "Today is ours."

"Ireland, Ireland, here I come," John said, holding his hands up to heaven. Paddy was angry and told the world's press that judges couldn't dispense justice—they didn't know how to!

I approached the microphone in a daze of happiness and shock. I had dreamed about this moment, what it would be like, what I would say. Yet the moment I came to speak I was just overjoyed. "I've spent sixteen years in prison, but justice has been done today. I'd like to thank all the people everywhere who helped us. Thank you very much." I stood there for a few seconds just looking in bewilderment at the crowds. Many of the people behind the barriers were in tears.

Our relatives ran towards us after we finished speaking. It was a moment in my life I shall never forget. I watched Dick's children run to him, hugging and embracing him, Billy's daughter Breda greeting her dad, Paddy's son Seán, and Tracy Hunter grabbing hold of Gerry's hand in absolute delight.

Gareth didn't appear at all in front of the cameras, nor did Tony Gifford or Mike Mansfield. I saw them briefly standing at the door of the Bailey, serene and happy. Gareth was not just a brilliant lawyer but a wonderful human being, renowned for her modesty. I rarely saw a picture of her in any newspaper. She wouldn't be appearing today either; but our gratitude to her was immeasurable.

Standing outside the Old Bailey, dazed with so many mixed emotions, I thought briefly of Lancaster, when the six of us were the most hated men in England. Today we were the victors.

We were taken to a big house in Hampstead, a rather exclusive part of London, where Father Gilmore had arranged for us to be received in private. It was a wonderful drive on a lovely spring day. We arrived in advance of the mini-buses, and were offered tea and sandwiches, beer, and champagne. Photographs were taken by the only paper allowed in, at our request, the *Irish Post*. Their coverage of our plight and the editor's unshakable belief in our innocence gave a great boost to our families years before the rest of the press took up the torch.

We spent time out in the garden while waiting for our families to arrive. We were like children; we took turns on a child's swing. In the house I went around touching everything, going from room to room. It seemed so strange, so different to be in a house again. The walls and ceilings of the rooms seemed close. There were soft chairs, carpets, and comfort everywhere.

Eileen, Patsy and Noel were not at court for my release. They had evaded publicity throughout my whole sixteen years, and still couldn't face it now. As in 1975, when I was convicted, they watched the events on television; but this time it wasn't through a shop window but surrounded by family and friends—the Mulready family, who lived in London. Geraldine and Arthur remained in Birmingham to take care of their daughter. I had spoken to Eileen and Geraldine by phone the night before; Geraldine told me she would video our release for me, and we arranged to meet in a week's time and have a private family reunion.

Bishop Daly describes our release in a way that I would want to express it myself: "a day of sheer unadulterated joy and relief that ultimately the truth has emerged and the innocence of these men has been proclaimed for the world to see."

Patsy was in tears, clutching a handkerchief and laughing at the same time. Eileen smiled, looking very happy, if a little tired. She was over sixty now, and it had been a long journey. She just said, "Thank God it's all over." I hugged her, and we sat together with Patsy and Charlie, eating sandwiches and drinking tea. My nightmare had ended.

1 4

FREEDOM

Two celebrations were arranged for us on the first
night of our release. Billy, Paddy and John and their families
and friends joined Gareth and campaigners from throughout
England for a party at the Irish Centre in Camden Town,
London. The venue was most appropriate, as the centre had
facilitated the London group's meeting for the past six years. At
the same time a celebration was laid on by Granada Television's
World in Action team, who wanted to film us for an hour-long
programme to be shown later that week. Billy, Paddy and John
arranged to be filmed later, and the rest of us went with Granada.

We were taken by coach from Father Gilmore's house out
into the Berkshire countryside, where Gerry, Dick and I and our
families stayed for two nights in a hotel at Granada's expense.
You would have to cross over a bridge or swim a lake to reach
the hotel if you hadn't a pass. Several press people tried to get
by the security men; one photographer tried to swim the lake
and nearly drowned.

After sixteen years, rising at the crack of dawn was by now
habitual. On my first morning I woke up still in a dream, not
sure where I was. My mind was still in prison: I kept expecting

the door to be opened and a screw to appear. My freedom to open my hotel room door, to walk out and go anywhere I pleased required a huge mental adjustment after years without that simple right. I had my liberty, but I wasn't fully confident I knew how to use it. It would take me time, I knew, to come to terms with the fact that I could again make decisions for myself.

I told myself to take one step at a time, not to rush into anything. Every experience was new. The food and drink, the plush hotel surroundings, people being polite and pleasant to me—all of it was new. There was food in abundance, but it all appeared too rich after years of stodgy food. The night before at dinner I ate only the food I recognised: a few potatoes and a bit of meat and a nice dessert. I managed two pints of lager, drinking very slowly. Eileen, Patsy and Charlie were there to make sure I didn't overdo it.

My surroundings were in stark contrast to a harsh prison cell. Our room was luxurious, with its own bathroom, a phone by the bed, and a television that I could switch on or off or change channels on as I chose—a novelty for me. The furniture was comfortable and soft. The full-length mirrors took some getting used to, though. When I opened the wardrobe my own reflection startled me: I thought there was a screw in the room! When I looked out the hotel window there were no grey walls, no police dogs, no exercise yards, no barbed wire, no men in prison uniform, just a beautiful view of the countryside as far as the eye could see.

I decided to take a stroll round the grounds before breakfast. From the moment I woke up I still expected to be directed, to be told where to go. Used to seeking permission for almost every normal activity a person at liberty enjoys, my instinct was to get the okay from the hotel porters or receptionists to go for a walk! I got dressed quickly and made my way out to the grounds hurriedly in case anyone might stop me. Just after eight o'clock I took my first walk as a free man. It's impossible to describe the pleasure and happiness I felt at that moment. To be free to walk in a park or along a country road was what I wanted most of all. Some of the lads wanted to walk in the rain, others to see the sky at night; a walk in the countryside, to be part of nature for a short while, was my dearest wish. The spring flowers were just beginning to blossom; there were beautiful delicate spring colours everywhere, green trees and greener lawns, a little bridge leading to woods further on—you could walk for miles. There was silence and peace everywhere. The only sound was that of the birds singing. The joy of just being able to walk, to go as far as I wished and begin to experience the freedom I now had was intense. I could have walked for hours that morning. I didn't want it to end.

Sitting on a seat watching the swans and ducks on the lake, I remembered when I used to take Geraldine's hand and we would go to feed the ducks together at a small lake near our house in Birmingham. For the first time I felt peaceful. The horror and the nightmare world I lived in for sixteen years passed before me. I would never have to return to that life again. This was a dream come true, my idea of paradise. I hardly noticed the television crew, who were filming my every move. One of them interrupted my thoughts when he walked up close behind me and made me jump. "Christ, I thought you were a screw!" "You'll be all right now," he said. "You're free. You can go where you like."

I felt like singing that morning at the top of my voice. I was really happy.

I returned for breakfast feeling great. The hotel restaurant was full of our people, all laughing and joking, ploughing through the morning papers, cracking jokes about this picture and that headline. It must have been an amazing sight for the staff. The night before at the meal many of them were moved by our presence and the happiness of families reunited, and some were in tears.

The main photographs in all the papers were those capturing our exit from the Old Bailey. "Freedom for the Six," ran the headlines; "Innocent"; "Grand exit greeted by wild scenes of rejoicing"; "Twenty-one murder convictions fall after sixteen years"; "Release of the Six forces Royal Commission on entire criminal justice system." The *Irish Independent* said simply, "A hundred thousand welcomes." There was an excellent picture of Paddy pointing his finger at the Court of Appeal with an angry look on his face; there was one of me being embraced by a journalist with several people in the crowd reaching out. The *Daily Telegraph*, renowned for its support for the establishment, joined in the press jubilation, without going overboard of course. "When they came out, they fairly bounced out of the doors, but still looking like a group of likely lads who set off for a weekend in Ireland in November 1974 and never made it."

The *Sun*, predictably, ran a story about our likely compensation—we would become "millionaires overnight." Its editorial commented that we would again be "free to attend IRA funerals, free to go to Republican rallies, free to raise funds for the IRA," and so on. The *Birmingham Post* ran a story, "What about the victims?" which of course was fair comment.

All Dick's grandchildren stayed in the hotel for the two nights. It was amazing to see him going across the grounds of the hotel surrounded by his children and grandchildren; you could see the happiness on all their faces and the pride Dick felt in his lovely young family.

Charlie took over the night's celebrations in the bar the second evening. He always had a fine voice, and he simply couldn't stop singing. I was amazed; not since my young days had I heard Charlie in such fine form. He stole the show. I managed two pints of lager again. The food was rich and very tasty, but I still wasn't used to it yet.

For two days the television crew were there the whole time, though given the circumstances they were very understanding of the feelings of men just released from prison. They did their job well. We completed all the interviews, which were sometimes gruelling. Surrounded by such beauty, we had nevertheless to relive for the programme some harrowing experiences. I was glad to get it over with.

We left the Granada people promising to keep in touch, and Eileen and I headed for the bright lights of London. I almost ran out of the underground when we alighted to go to the famous Oxford Street shopping district. I was afraid, and going underground brought me instantly back to the dungeons of my early years in prison. I felt suffocated, but Eileen was reassuring. "You'll be okay. Just relax." Relax! I was sweating, terrified. The tube was packed; passengers stood too close to each other. The escalator was equally terrifying. I couldn't believe how people would want to run up it: surely it was travelling fast enough as it was. The pace of everything and everybody made my head whirl. I didn't think it could be possible to get used to this kind of travel.

Walking round the big stores, I must have appeared to the shop assistants like someone from another planet. The stores were large, impersonal places. People approached us with funny voices: "Can I help you, sir?" The "sir" bit made me laugh! We spent money on jackets, trousers, and various other items, and it came to over two hundred pounds—another big surprise. I couldn't get over how expensive everything was: I was used to wages of four pounds a week.

I could never have made such a trip without Eileen. Simply crossing the road was a terrifying ordeal for me. The streets were crowded with shoppers. I felt claustrophobic, yet keen to see everything around me; I was like a child again, seeing the city lights for the first time. Needless to say, this wasn't my best experience so soon after my release. I wasn't sure if jumping in at the deep end was good for me or not. Eileen considered it probably was; she is usually right.

On my first Sunday afternoon Eileen and I were invited to Sunday dinner with the Mulready family in their large old house in Hackney in north London. This was my first visit to an ordinary family home since my release. The children of the house—Molly, Nora, Ned, and Séamie—surprised me with how much they knew about us and with their ready acceptance of me. We sat in the garden for a little while, surrounded by a clothes-line full of children's washing. The house was full of life and the pleasant noise of children's voices. It was a very nice feeling to be part of an ordinary family for a few hours; the sounds and smells of life on a lazy Sunday afternoon brought back so many memories to me. It was a lovely few hours, complete with a typical Sunday dinner of roast beef and Yorkshire pudding. I felt completely relaxed, and dozed off in the chair with the Sunday papers on my knee, just as I did in my own home all those years ago.

On St Patrick's night we went to the Irish Centre, and I had the pleasure of buying my first round of drinks. I was given a great welcome, and was called on to make a speech. As I'm not very good at speeches I offered to sing a song instead. I sang "Danny Boy," and I could feel my voice rising with the happiness I felt. In years gone by it was something I always loved to do, but now to sing in front of a packed Irish centre on St Patrick's night really tested me. I must have shaken hands with at least two hundred people that night.

Standing in a pub in north London a few weeks later, I ordered three pints of Guinness. I tried to lift one of the pints off the counter. It was stuck. To my amusement and embarrassment I realised it was a model of a pint of Guinness. Such attractions weren't around in my days. I found myself in similar situations for a good few weeks. Later I stood back and observed a bit of protocol in pubs and at socials, especially wine and cheese affairs, before venturing to make any moves. I was a fast learner, and people were generally very considerate.

It was my intention to go back at some time to Birmingham, but I needed time to adjust to being back in society, and despite the fact that Eileen and Geraldine had continued to live in Birmingham I had very mixed feelings about returning. Eileen and I decided that for a few months at least it would be better to remain in London. For three months or so we stayed as the guests of Father Colm Ó Gallchóir from Gaoth Dobhair, County Donegal, the parish priest of a working-class parish in north London. I liked him instantly; we became good friends, and I spent a pleasant three months going places I never expected to see and meeting people I had only read about or seen on television.

Meeting Jack Charlton and the Irish team on the Wembley pitch was something I could only have dreamed about. Colm arranged for it to become a reality; his brother was a broadcaster with Raidió na Gaeltachta and he was there to cover the match. We went early on Monday morning to watch the team in a training session. Journalists from the Irish papers recognised me, and soon the English papers joined in. They asked me if I would like to meet Jack Charlton and the Irish team; I said I would be honoured, but given the importance of the event I didn't think it was on. However, much to my surprise and delight I found myself being introduced to the team by Jack Charlton. Before introducing me, in his typical direct fashion he said to me, "You've had a rough time." I smiled and just said, "It's all over now." As I was introduced to the members of the team, to their surprise I named the League team each one played for. When I came to Paul McGrath I said to him, "You play for my team, Aston Villa." Ray Houghton, who was just along the line, commented, "Yes, but they were a better team before he went there!"

The follow-up was the journey on the tube to Wembley two nights later, which unnerved me a little. The train was packed with Irish and English supporters. A very excited Irish supporter announced my presence; I was cheered along, but one Englishman approached me to ask very directly, "What were you doing at that funeral then?" I didn't respond, and I was very grateful that Colm was there. We got up at the next stop and changed carriages. I tried not to let it spoil the game for me, but it was a taste of the hostility that was still around.

I got my long-wished-for day at the races when Colm took Eileen, Sister Joan Kane and me to Kempton Park. I thought I was an expert at putting on the bets, but Eileen well and truly beat me. It was a beautiful sunny day and the whole atmosphere on the track was exciting. The last time I was on a track was in 1959. It was a lovely day out, and I thought of Cyril Birkett, my old prison mate and betting partner. If he could see me now!

Geraldine and Arthur came with my granddaughter to see me in London a week after my release, and we had a beautiful reunion in the privacy of Colm's home. My first walk with Geraldine in the streets was pleasant and very natural. We walked along together chatting as we used to do every day long ago. We did a bit of shopping; everything was calm and peaceful, and it was nice to be close to her again. Arthur and I went to the local in the evening and enjoyed a good drink. It was a lovely few days. They returned to Birmingham, and Eileen and I made arrangements as soon as I felt able to go and visit them there.

A London inmate had told me I would be out in time to see a great show in the West End: an American production of *Show Boat* was coming to the London Palladium. I had seen the film with Paul Robeson dozens of times over the years, knew all the songs, and used to sing some of them at home with the others. It was a show I would have given anything to see. My luck was in, and we got tickets. We enjoyed it enormously—just being at the Palladium was a marvellous experience. While we were standing in the aisles waiting to leave, an English gentleman came over to our seats, shook hands warmly, and said, "Well done! I was rooting for you for years." It was completely unexpected in a place like this. Others began to look in our direction, and a few gave thumbs-up signs or smiled kindly.

Walking back through the streets of London's famous West End, I was shocked by the sight of several young people lying on the cold pavement, on the steps of the BBC building in Regent Street, and in the doorways of big stores. They had bits of blankets around them and looked as if they were settling in to sleep there for the night. As we moved on I saw others, including a very old tramp who could hardly move, rooting in a dustbin. No-one seemed to notice. The night was very cold and frosty. I was horrified to learn that this was common in London in 1992. Even in prison a man could shelter from the cold! The obvious indifference of all the people passing by, not even glancing their way, said it all: a society that didn't give a toss. No wonder it was possible for people to rot in prison.

We had extraordinary good luck when we were helped to find a very comfortable flat in north London. I now possessed the keys to my own home; I could open and shut my front door as I pleased. It's amazing how I ever took such simple rights, part of the everyday life of a free man, so much for granted. Eileen had the best organising ways of anyone I know, and within two weeks of moving into the flat she had made it into a very comfortable, elegant home, beautifully furnished with every comfort I could wish for, including teletext on the telly—an essential for a man studying the daily race card. Eileen returned for a while to Geraldine in Birmingham, and for the first time I faced the challenge of coping on my own, organising and controlling my own life after sixteen years of being directed and instructed. I could really and truly do absolutely as I pleased. Contemplating that thought a few hours after Eileen went up to Birmingham, I set out for the supermarket, calling in to the bookie's on the way, having first read the form in the *Sporting Life*.

It was with some bewilderment and amusement that I got used to being recognised in the street. Living in north London in a predominantly Irish area, I started to enjoy going to the local pubs, making friends and mixing with my own people. The Irish community was well established, with several welfare agencies available to help. There were few places Irish people could go for help before I went inside; indeed if there had been, all our families might have got the support they desperately needed. Irish centres like the one in Birmingham did the best they could. I recall some of our women going to Father Paddy Sheridan in the Birmingham Irish Centre for help after their windows were broken and their houses ransacked. He worked alone and did the best he could, but God knows how difficult that must have been in the aftermath of the explosions. Irish people everywhere were afraid to lift their heads.

The Irish centres now provided a place to sit and relax in in comfort and dignity; gone were the rough, run-down clubs and pubs we all accepted as good enough one time. On the political front, Irish people I met appeared much more aware of their rights. Information on the Prevention of Terrorism Act and other issues was available in almost all Irish venues. What happened to us could happen again; but I feel that our people are much more attuned on their legal rights and couldn't be pushed around or terrorised as we were without someone or some organisation becoming involved immediately.

On my first summer out I went to several Irish festivals in London, the biggest one, held in the heart of the Irish community in west London, attracting ninety thousand people. To be just an Irishman among several thousands having a family day out was a wonderful experience. I had a good few pints, and spent the day just observing the spectacle and feeling emotionally charged, sometimes on the verge of tears. I stood with about thirty thousand people listening to Daniel O'Donnell singing old songs I had heard in my childhood. All the crowd were singing with him. People who recognised me shook hands with me and expressed their delight that I was able to share this day with them. They had no idea what it meant to me to be just one of them again. At the Comhaltas Ceoltóirí stage I listened in amazement at the talent of hundreds of London Irish children playing traditional Irish music. I sat with the parents and talked about the rich and satisfying life these children had. How good it was to see them master our own music!

At a similar though smaller event I was invited on stage to be welcomed by the crowd. I couldn't speak, overcome by the welcome I received. Dermot Hegarty and his merry band accompanied me in a song; I almost ran off the stage afterwards. Their manager later offered to help me record a tape, which I may well do some day.

Ordinary tasks of everyday life continued to be difficult. I hated crossing busy roads or standing in queues for buses or in the post office. I just felt like running away. Going to deal with bureaucracies, filling in forms and the like presented their own embarrassments. When I got my new home I tried to get my electricity connected at the local electricity board. Eileen was with me. I was grilled about my previous address. "We have to have it before we give you a supply, otherwise you'll have to pay a £100 deposit." The whole conversation took place at the counter in front of other customers. I just wanted to leave, but Eileen was more patient than me. We needed the electricity, and Eileen in the end said we would come back later.

I kept up my daily routine of walking, as I had every day of my life in prison. Walking in the park one day, one of the priests from Colm's parish, Bernie Costello, remarked to me how I always stuck to the boundary. "You can walk on the grass, you know. You can even go in a straight line if you wish."

I signed up with a very good Irish doctor, who understood

straight away what I had been through once I told him who I was. He embraced me and offered me whatever help he could give at any time. He suggested I should carry on walking and exercising, and if frustration set in—which he advised was bound to happen—to perhaps go into a gym and punch a bag. I saw him frequently in my first few weeks. Dr Kinsella was in my view the ideal doctor for a man trying to make his way in a new world full of complexities he had not grown used to. He had a sense of humour too, and liked a good chat. Being used to very formal and distant prison doctors, I found him a breath of fresh air.

In May all six of us went to Dublin and were taken through the streets in an open-top CIE bus. Thousands of people came to greet us. We stopped in front of the GPO, and each of us in turn was introduced and received a tremendous welcome. Gerry and I discussed how we didn't like making speeches. If I could have got away with it I would have preferred to sing a song, but somehow the throngs of people wanted to hear us all speak. In the end I said what was most natural to me and what was in my heart. "I am very happy to be back in my own country again." It was a wonderful moment. I thought back to the scenes we saw of the Parade of Innocence and the great warmth of the Dublin people. It was a great joy to be able to personally thank them for their years of support. John was similarly welcomed when he returned to Derry. The people turned out in their hundreds to greet the coach that took the entire Walker family home. John had dreamed only of that moment when we were together in Long Lartin.

We had tea with the newly elected President, Mary Robinson; to be invited to the home of the President of Ireland was a great honour. She encouraged us to relax, which was a little difficult sitting on six high seats facing the President. But Paddy, never one to be overawed by big occasions, was quickly on familiar terms and calling her Mary. He was a natural, easy talker. I told her that Eileen came from Mayo and how pleasing it was that a Mayo woman got the job. Her staff were extremely hospitable and made us very welcome.

Many people asked me after my release if I would go back to Birmingham. It was with some trepidation that I thought of returning. I wondered how I would be received. My feelings were not, of course, those of a man with a guilty conscience, but nevertheless I was aware that many people who believed the courts when they condemned us still chose to believe in our guilt, even though the same courts had cleared our names. From the hundreds of people who wrote to us I knew also about the work carried out on our behalf by many good Birmingham people who believed in our innocence. Eileen had continued to live quietly in her home, troubling nobody and in turn being disturbed by no-one. Geraldine and Arthur were settled and content with their lives on the outskirts of the city. My arrival on the scene wouldn't be easy. Nevertheless I wanted to go, just to see the place again. Birmingham had been my adopted home since 1947. My family—my wife, my daughter, my son-in-law and granddaughter—all lived there. I wanted to visit their homes.

On the way up on the train my nerves were a bit on edge. How would I cope if people in the streets reacted against me? I never learnt to wholly accept hostility towards me.

New Street Station was, of course, completely changed. The Taurus Bar, where the six of us had that fatal pint, had gone.

A cold shudder ran through me standing on a platform waiting to continue our journey to where Geraldine and Arthur lived. But I stayed calm and hoped I wouldn't be recognised. I just wanted to get to my destination quickly, to adjust at my leisure to being back in Birmingham in the security and privacy of my daughter's home.

Arthur was a first-class gentleman. "You are always welcome here." He shook my hand warmly; I immediately relaxed. My granddaughter sat on my lap and we got to know each other a bit better. Their home was comfortable, with an air of contentment and happiness. Arthur had a great sense of humour. We got on very well, striking into an immediate discussion about football. He himself had the reputation of being an excellent footballer, and played two or three times a week. Despite all that had happened, Geraldine had done well. Both had successful careers; Arthur was a rising star at his work and regarded as very successful, considering he was still only in his late twenties. I left their house that evening with a lovely warm feeling. My daughter was happy. Something in my life had gone right.

Eileen's home for the past ten years was a small terrace house on a council estate built in the 1960s. The rooms were small but warm and comfortable, without any particular luxuries. I noticed several ornaments and soft toys around the place that men in prison had made for me and that Eileen had kept.

I knew Erdington well before I went inside. I used to go to several of the pubs in the area, as well as the clubs. Eileen encouraged me to go out for a walk. "You have to get used to it some time." It was a warm summer day; the cap and glasses I wore to disguise myself were hot and sweaty. I knew the streets, the shops so well. It was strange to have to walk these familiar paths in disguise. I realised on my first walk out on the streets, feeling as uncomfortable as I did and full of nervous anxiety, that after all things would never be the same for me here. I could never live in Birmingham again.

I wasn't recognised in a pub that used to be one of my old haunts. I had a quiet drink, spoke to no-one, just observed the people and the place. It was a shadow of its former self, a run-down pub with old furnishings and no atmosphere at all.

The first person I spoke to in a Birmingham pub was, ironically, the last person I spoke to before my arrest, Charlie Sloane, my old mate from Belfast. We both remarked on the coincidence of this meeting after almost seventeen years. We later carried on to another club, where I met a few more people I once knew. Brian Kearney assured me that "we were all for you here. None of us believed any of you did it." Brian told me he had never expected to see me again. I spent a pleasant few hours with them, going over old times, catching up on people and places that had gone. The governor in the club made me welcome, so it can't have been too bad.

Later I met an old neighbour, a Brummie working-class man who lived in the little street from where I was taken that night in 1974. He recognised me and threw his arms around me, expressing heartfelt sorrow at what happened to me and all the others. "I'm surprised you want to come back here. As a matter of fact I wouldn't be surprised if you didn't want to live in this country again after what they did to you." He often thought about me, he said, and never expected to see me again. I was chuffed by his welcome and his genuine feelings. Probably many more Birmingham people felt as he did.

I always wanted to go back to Villa Park to watch a football match. I had my opportunity in October 1992 when friends invited me along. It was Manchester United v. Aston Villa. I skipped along like a youth to the match, running yards ahead of my friends. I couldn't wait to get into the grounds. Just about everything had changed, and for the better. The seating was more comfortable, no queue or mad rush at the gates, plenty of stewards around, good floodlighting, but the atmosphere I remembered so well was still there. There had always been a special family feeling about the place, and that was the same. The price of tickets was a surprise, but I could see that the money was being put to good use. The grounds were well kept, the place comfortable and safe. The great game of football doesn't change, it just gets better and the players more skilled.

I have since been back to Birmingham several times, though I have not made my home there. Eileen retains many of the good friends who helped her or that she made since I went inside. I visit Geraldine's, and I have become closer to my little granddaughter, who gives me great pleasure as I watch her growing up and beginning to talk. I enjoy visiting Birmingham, and gradually the fears and anxieties about being recognised are fading, though I remain cautious.

On a cold January day in 1992 Arthur lost his life in a pile-up on a fog-bound motorway. He was only thirty, fit and active. His death totally devastated Geraldine, leaving her alone with a fourteen-month-old daughter and another child on the way. No-one knows the grief that Geraldine felt. Who can explain the reason why such a terrible tragedy should befall a woman who had experienced so much sadness in her young life already.

Arthur was a very special person who achieved a great deal and touched many people's hearts in his short lifetime. He was full of life, a wonderful husband and father, destined to have a great and successful life. To Geraldine he was her life. Her happiness was bound up in his. They had a very special relationship and were blissfully happy together. A perfect match. Made in Heaven, you might say.

Arthur always supported Geraldine, despite the fact that I was convicted of the Birmingham pub bombings and labelled a "bomber." He always believed in my innocence, having read as far back as 1975 *The Birmingham Framework*. He had already drawn his own conclusions about our innocence before he ever met Geraldine.

Arthur himself knew tragedy in his early life when his mother died. He was reared by his father, whom he regarded as a very special man. He was devoted to his father and in many ways could understand how Geraldine must have felt about my imprisonment. Arthur always comforted, supported and encouraged Geraldine. He brought happiness back into her life. No-one could ever replace him.

It is hard to fathom why a person should have to suffer so much grief. Geraldine has her own philosophy about it. She believes we are all given a cross to bear and must carry on and do the best we can, regardless of the load.

Eileen knew Arthur better than I did. She suffered his loss acutely. His death shattered all our lives, but our love and respect for him will never die. His great sense of humour and fine personal qualities and caring nature will live in our memories for ever.

One of Arthur's greatest wishes was to have a son, someone to share his love of football. Six months after he died Geraldine gave birth to a baby boy. These two beautiful children are a constant and happy reminder of Arthur and are a guarantee his memory will live on in a positive and fruitful way. My lasting thoughts about Arthur will always be concerned with the joy and happiness he gave Geraldine in the few short years they had together.

After twenty years I returned to Belfast in June 1992, a year and three months after my release. My good friend Séamus Kelters of the *Irish News* picked me up at Dublin Airport on a beautiful June evening. We went by car, a first for me: all my previous journeys between Belfast and Dublin were by coach or train. It took several hours, giving me time to adjust to the prospect of returning to my home town after so long. This was to be a very private, quick visit; I just wanted to be with my family and to spend a bit of time in Ardoyne with old friends.

Séamus took me the long way round, by Carlingford Lough and up along the County Down coast, through some of the most spectacular scenery in Ireland. He made sure we avoided the main checkpoints on the border, to my enormous relief.

Going through the fishing village of Kilkeel, I remembered as a youth going there often with the wagon when I worked in the bottle factory. The village I remembered had not changed much. Coming nearer to Belfast I noticed all the red, white and blue bunting and the pavements painted with the Union Jack in preparation for the Twelfth of July. It was strange to see this after so many years away, but obviously, like Séamus, if you lived there you would take these old symbols of the past for granted.

I spent my first evening with Séamus's mother and father. We talked about old times, going over famous events and people we knew, and reminiscing about old Belfast Celtic footballers. They remarked that I hadn't lost my accent very much. I felt at home with this lovely couple: they were the kind of Belfast people I grew up with. Séamus's father and I went to get the papers in the local newsagent next morning. I remarked that I had a free copy of the *Irish News* in prison for years.

Séamus took me to meet all the people at the *Irish News* office. We drove from Andersonstown through the city, and I was amazed at the changes I saw. Apart from some immovable landmarks like the City Hall and the Mater Hospital, the whole place had changed dramatically. Old shops were gone, there was massive redevelopment; several buildings I knew as a child were derelict, either bombed out or just left to deteriorate. The armoured cars and British soldiers on the streets, the ramps everywhere and the graffiti on the walls, all gave the appearance of a city I hardly knew.

In the *Irish News* offices I was delighted to meet so many people I had either spoken to over the years by phone or who had from time to time written to me or written about us. The editor, Nick Gorbett, and the owner, John Fitzpatrick, gave me a terrific welcome and laid on a lunch for me. Another good character who used to write for the paper came back specially to see me, Peter Montellier, an old man now. I also met Hugh Russell, an Olympic gold medallist in boxing. I surprised him with how much I knew about his famous win; he surprised me by telling me he was one of the many photographers outside the Old Bailey on the day of my release and had been delighted to get the picture that his paper ran. I had a lovely few hours there. I asked Séamus for the originals of the stories I used to send in, but he told me they were kept by the staff in the printing department as souvenirs, which made me laugh and was very flattering.

Patsy, Noel and Dan lived just outside north Belfast, high on the hills overlooking Belfast. It was a little way from Ardoyne, but from the top of the hill here you could see right down into the city. The house was small and comfortable. Patsy prepared a beautiful tea, and we had a wonderful, nostalgic few hours before we went by bus down into Ardoyne. There Patsy left me with some old friends at the Star club. I was quickly recognised and given a warm welcome, and too much to drink. I had intended to stay just an hour or so in the club, but there were so many people I wanted to see.

That night Patsy, Noel and I sat up talking till two in the morning. We remarked on how lovely the house was, and how different from years ago, when life was so hard. Dan came in too, and I was delighted that he recognised me and spoke to me. He looked well. He understood perfectly the significance of my return home, even if he didn't express it as we would. I know Patsy would like me to have stayed longer, but there would be other times.

People were asking for me to call in to them, but I had little time to see everyone I wanted to see. I visited Jean and Denis Murphy; they had been so good to me, and now here I was in Jean's home surrounded by her family. Jean's daughter did me a special favour and took me to see my old friend Paddy Cassidy. Paddy was ill now and immobile, but he had kept in touch for years through our letters. We talked about old times, and Paddy had all the news about others we used to know. But watching him struggle through his illness made me sad. He was clearly in pain; and despite my sixteen years in prison I felt I couldn't endure what Paddy was going through now and with the courage he showed for my sake. I left promising to stay longer the next time.

Séamus drove me back to Dublin, but our passage through

the border was not completely uneventful. Séamus was asked to open the boot and to open my case. I was very edgy and just stared ahead of me, hoping not to be recognised. On top of my case was a photograph of John Walker surrounded by well-wishers, which Séamus gave me to give to John, whom I had arranged to meet in Dublin. The RUC man asked Séamus who it was. "That's John Walker, one of the Birmingham Six, and I have another one in the car." The policeman immediately ushered the car on, with lots of encouraging information about checkpoints to avoid.

My visit to Belfast was short and hectic. I would definitely be back again, though not to live there. I had been away too long.

I spent a hilarious few days with a good friend in Dublin, Déaglán Moynihan, a rare man, who talked endlessly and made me laugh. He had a great understanding of how I felt after I returned from Belfast. Later I went down to his home in Mullingar, where I spent a lovely week with his brother Colmán and his wife, Sheila. They were warm, hospitable people, like the town itself. It is my wish to end my days in Ireland, and I could think of few places I would like better than Mullingar, which is just big enough to accept a stranger like me looking for a place to rest and be at peace. They have a very good dog track as well!

I am often asked if I feel bitter about my experiences. I usually respond by saying no. Bitterness, it seems to me, eats out the heart and soul of a man. It can destroy a human being. I tried very hard in prison not to allow myself to become bitter. However, I do feel a great sadness at the futility of it all.

I have always said that the planting of bombs in pubs or in

any public places is a horrendous act. It solves nothing, and brings pain and suffering to innocent people. The Birmingham explosions took the lives of twenty-one innocent people, and more than 150 were injured or maimed for life. I have deep sympathy for the victims and their families. However, we too were victims. In their haste to punish somebody for the terrible carnage inflicted on so many innocent people that night in 1974, the police picked on us. We were six innocent people whom they beat and tortured into making false confessions. We spent sixteen years behind bars for a crime we didn't commit. Our homes were destroyed. Our families were left in disarray; our children's futures were shattered. The mighty and the powerful could not bring themselves to admit that they were wrong. Justice was sacrificed for sixteen years to protect reputations. Our lives can never know normality again. It is my wish that out of the suffering inflicted on six innocent human beings people in high places responsible for our imprisonment, and who denied the truth for sixteen years, will learn by their mistakes, show some contrition and above all else ensure that such an injustice will never happen again. The evidence before my eyes and on the faces of many innocent people I left behind on the day I was released from prison suggests that it may be a very long learning process. As I conclude my story, the grief and suffering caused by such injustice and by the Birmingham bombings goes on. What was it all for?